WEEKNIGHT
VEGETARIAN

WEEKNIGHT VEGETARIAN

Easy vegetable recipes
for lunch & dinner

Joe Woodhouse
Kyle Books

Dedication

I would like to dedicate this book to anyone who cooks from scratch.

Thanks

It takes a team to make a book. I am extremely grateful for the support and help from everyone involved in creating this one.

To my wife Olia, for her honest and enthusiastic feedback, and to my family, for eating the various trials, tests and iterations of all the recipes.

To Emily Sweet, for always giving considered and solid advice. It is massively appreciated, thank you.

To Jo Copestick, for shaping this book to become what it is. It has been a joy to work with you on it.

To Juliette Norsworthy, whose advice and input I always value. I was extremely happy to have you working on this book.

To Leanne Bryan, for keeping me on track in the best possible way. I have really enjoyed working with you, thank you.

To the rest of the team at Kyle Books. Each book is a different experience and it gets better every time. Thank you.

To Lucy Bannell, for making my text make sense, for your enthusiasm about the recipes and for being the first person to cook from the book!

To Helen Bratby, for making my books look their best. It is always such a pleasure to see your work.

Thank you to everyone who gets a copy of any of my books, and to those who make and enjoy the recipes. It really means the world to me when I see people cooking recipes from my books.

Finally, thank you to anyone who has skills and knowledge and takes the time to teach someone else, passing on techniques in a gentle and reassuring manner to help others.

First published in Great Britain in 2026 by Kyle Books, an imprint of Octopus Publishing Group Ltd, Carmelite House, 50 Victoria Embankment, London EC4Y 0DZ www.octopusbooks.co.uk

An Hachette UK Company
www.hachette.co.uk

The authorized representative in the EEA is Hachette Ireland, 8 Castlecourt Centre, Dublin 15, D15 XTP3, Ireland (email: info@hbgi.ie)

Text copyright © Joe Woodhouse 2026
Photography copyright © Joe Woodhouse 2026

Distributed in the US by Hachette Book Group, 1290 Avenue of the Americas, 4th and 5th Floors, New York, NY 10104

Distributed in Canada by Canadian Manda Group, 664 Annette St., Toronto, Ontario, Canada M6S 2C8

All rights reserved. No part of this work may be reproduced or utilized in any form or by any means, electronic or mechanical, including photocopying, recording or by any information storage and retrieval system, without the prior written permission of the publisher.

Joe Woodhouse asserts the moral right to be identified as the author of this work.

UK ISBN: 9781804194041
US ISBN: 9781804193471
eISBN: 9781804193488

A CIP catalogue record for this book is available from the British Library.

Printed and bound in China.

10 9 8 7 6 5 4 3 2 1

Publisher: Joanna Copestick
Art Director & illustrator: Juliette Norsworthy
Designer: Helen Bratby
Senior Editor: Leanne Bryan
Copyeditor: Lucy Bannell
Photographer, food & prop stylist: Joe Woodhouse
Production Controllers: Lucy Carter & Nic Jones

6 Introduction

9 ASSEMBLY JOBS (mostly)
34 Your storecupboard essentials

37 MIX & MAKE
76 On seasoning

79 ONE POT ON THE HOB
118 Kids and other nervous eaters

121 IN & OUT OF THE OVEN
166 Cooking dried beans. Yes, on a weeknight

169 WORTH THE WASHING-UP
204 Batch-cooking: the über-hack

206 Index

208 About the Author | UK/US Terms

INTRODUCTION

I am a firm believer that you can eat well even when short on time. With a little forethought, you can eat very well every day, weaving interesting food into your week and not just waiting for those days when you have the luxury of more time. In this book, you'll find recipes that are fun, and engaging to make as well as to eat.

A large part of eating well – the way I like to do it, at least – is a little preparation. For example, having a trusty staple, such as beans, soaked or even batch-cooked, ready and waiting. As a lifelong lover of leftovers, I tend to lean towards making double or extra at each meal, in order to have something squirrelled away for later in the week when I know I will have little time. You will recognize that impulse in a lot of the dishes in this book, which can be batch-cooked, so you can portion up future quick lunches or dinners after you've eaten. Once you have worked a visit to the market or shops into your weekend plans, you will have the necessary tools at your disposal to do the same.

For some of these recipes, you may feel you need to concentrate when you first cook them, so set those aside to try when you know you'll have the time. But most of them take only minutes to assemble or make. All of them, I hope, will become adapted to fit your tastes or needs. If you don't have a certain ingredient, as always, sub in something you do, or even prefer. Have a play. Food should be fun, not stressful.

It does feel – in these days of rushing around and being constantly plugged in – that we have started to lose the art of slowing down. But taking the time to cook for yourself, or for those who you love, is a sacred practice. It's crucial, now more than ever, to set time aside for that. Time spent in the kitchen can be a meditation; a way to balance yourself and reset. Prioritize it, as well as those moments around the table, eating with your household, even on a Wednesday night in February. Food provides energy and balance, comfort and pleasure.

By building an arsenal of supporting ingredients, you can grease the wheels of flavour. A trusty extra virgin olive oil, a decent wine vinegar, favourite spices and a finishing salt will make even a slice of tomato on toast transcendent. It is worth seeking out elements that you really like and leaning into them.

The same can be said for often-overlooked base ingredients, such as grains or beans. I will simply soak and cook a bowlful of either and have them there, waiting, in the fridge. Beans can be thrown into a spicy tomato sauce for a chilli, or mixed into a soup, giving not just bulk but nutrients, too. Grains are quickly tossed with egg and veg for a fried rice, or simply serve as a bonus carb that you don't have to cook to round out a meal. It is worth noting that the better the quality of the ingredient, the less it needs tampering with. Try and get the best you can, supporting small and local growers or makers if possible.

I will say it again: have fun. Cooking, for me at least, is what life is about. So even if it's not quite that for you, I urge you to take it on with a little of the same passion. Run with it and experiment. Adapt it to you and yours. Eat together when possible, and always – always – eat to enjoy. Eat to your tastes, but try other tastes too... you never know, you might discover something wonderful. But, primarily, EAT WELL. You deserve it, any time of the week.

ASSEMBLY JOBS (mostly)

These recipes range from simply combining storecupboard ingredients in a bowl and you're done to putting those odds and ends in the veg drawer to creative use or using a minimum of cooking to maximum effect. Any which way, they won't break the bank in terms of time invested. Think something tasty to grab just before or as you rush out the door in the morning, or something worthwhile for dinner without too much effort.

TOTAL TIME: **25 MINUTES**

Jewelled couscous

I wanted to give you a dish that is not only a great lunchbox filler but that can also hold its own at the dinner table. Use a single nut if you like, or swap in what you prefer or have to hand, but do have a play with how you would like the nuts to be spiced. I favour a really good curry powder, as I don't have to think too much about it and it adds a lovely layer of flavour from the warming spices. Lots of texture and taste is key here.

Make the stock at the last possible minute, for best results. SERVES 4.

- 300g (10½oz) couscous
- 1 tablespoon extra virgin olive oil
- finely grated zest and juice of 1 lemon
- 325ml (11fl oz) hot freshly made stock
- 200g (7oz) cavolo nero, or kale, or cabbage, leaves only, shredded
- 50g (1¾oz) unsalted butter (or 50ml/2fl oz olive oil works fine)
- 50g (1¾oz) almonds, roughly chopped, or to taste
- 50g (1¾oz) walnuts, broken into small pieces, or to taste
- 50g (1¾oz) shelled unsalted pistachios, or to taste
- 1 tablespoon curry powder (or see recipe introduction)
- 50g (1¾oz) dried cranberries, or dried cherries, or to taste
- 10g (¼oz) parsley, finely chopped, or to taste
- 100g (3½oz) pomegranate seeds, or to taste
- couple of pinches of chilli flakes (optional)
- salt

1. Find a large heatproof mixing bowl that will fit everything, as well as a tight-fitting lid or large-enough plate to cover it fully. Tip in the couscous and the oil, with a pinch of salt. Mix this around – I use a fork – until all the grains are coated lightly in oil. Stir in the lemon zest and juice, then the steaming-hot stock. Give it 2 turns with the fork, drop the cavolo nero, kale or cabbage leaves on top and cover.

2. Meanwhile, in a small saucepan, melt the butter and add the nuts with a pinch of salt. Cook over a medium–low heat, gently toasting the nuts until just golden. Just as they are done, add the curry powder, cook for a minute, then take off the heat.

3. After 15 minutes, the couscous should be ready. Fluff it with a fork while incorporating the cavolo nero, kale or cabbage leaves, nuts and remaining ingredients and mix to combine well. Taste, then top up any ingredients you feel need more of a presence. Serve.

ASSEMBLY JOBS (MOSTLY)

TOTAL TIME: **10 MINUTES**

Sharp, speedy storecupboard bean salad

I make this a lot for my son's packed lunches and it has saved many a chaotic morning rush to prepare him a decent meal before we all hurry out of the door. I then make it for myself again later on, for my own lunch, as I could genuinely eat this (or a version of it) every day. My son loves punchy, briny, sharp flavours, so a lot of dishes get balanced with those, but feel free to substitute them with any additions you would like, bearing in mind that the base – indeed the ethos – of this salad is that it is made from shelf-stable ingredients. It keeps well in the fridge, too. SERVES 2

1. Combine all the ingredients in a bowl with chilli flakes, olive oil and vinegar to taste. Taste and adjust the salt and pepper to your liking.

2. Serve straight away, or leave the flavours to marry for 30 minutes or so.

- 2 × 400g (14oz) cans of beans and/or lentils, or 1 large (700g/1lb 9oz) jar (mixed are good here, or go for a solo variety, such as borlotti, haricot or red kidney), drained
- 16 olives (2 small handfuls; I like kalamata), pitted and torn into quarters
- 9 cornichons, or 2 gherkins, chopped
- 1 heaped tablespoon drained capers, either small (lilliput or non pareilles), or chopped if large
- 2 roasted red peppers from a jar, chopped
- small handful of pickled chillies (for homemade, see page 75), chopped (optional)
- handful of red or white pickled onions, sliced, from a jar (or for homemade, see page 89)
- chilli flakes, to taste
- olive oil, to taste
- vinegar (any you like), to taste
- salt and black pepper

ASSEMBLY JOBS (MOSTLY)

TOTAL TIME: **25 MINUTES**

Curried tahini, lentil & crunchy veg salad

This dish is really quick and easy to pull together and great for using up odds and ends in the veg drawer. Prep all the ingredients and mix in the dressing at the last minute, or take them both along, packed separately, to a party or barbecue. In either case, though, if you want to make the salad ahead of time and have it ready in the fridge, leave the tomatoes out and either fold them through when serving or put them on top. The curried tahini dressing here is equally lovely on lots of other dishes, as a spread in sandwiches or used as a dip. For something more substantial, eat this salad with an omelette, or slabs of Crispy Tofu (see page 159).
SERVES 4

1. Preheat the oven to 200°C/180°C fan (400°F), Gas Mark 6. Spead the cashews over a small baking tray and toast them for 10–12 minutes or until golden. Keep an eye on them so that they don't burn. Set aside to cool.

2. Put all the curried tahini dressing ingredients in a blender with a good pinch of salt and blitz until smooth. Save half in a sealed container in the fridge; it will keep well for a week.

3. When you're ready to serve, reserve a sprinkling of the cashews and mint leaves, then combine the rest of the ingredients with the dressing in a bowl, mixing well to marry everything. Serve with the reserved cashews and mint scattered on top.

- 50g (1¾oz) cashews
- 15g (½oz) soft herbs (I like mint here, but parsley, dill and coriander are all good), roughly chopped
- 250g (9oz) white cabbage, or red cabbage, shredded
- 200g (7oz) cherry tomatoes, halved
- 2 celery sticks, finely sliced
- 2 carrots, coarsely grated, or cut into fine batons
- 1 green or red chilli, finely chopped (optional)
- 3 × 400g (14oz) cans of green lentils, drained, or about 350g (12oz) dried lentils, cooked and drained (see page 156)

For the curried tahini dressing
- 200g (7oz) tahini
- 200ml (7fl oz) water
- 10g (¼oz) curry powder
- 1 small thumb of fresh root ginger, peeled and roughly chopped
- 1–2 garlic cloves
- finely grated zest and juice of 1 lemon
- salt

ASSEMBLY JOBS (MOSTLY)

TOTAL TIME: 30–35 MINUTES

Sesame-crusted rice paper dumplings

A family favourite in our house, these dumplings also lend themselves to a production line if others want to lend a hand, so they're satisfying to make and eat alike. The toasted sesame coating makes them extremely addictive. Please have a play with fillings: a version heavy on the pickled shiitake front (see page 60) would be great. MAKES 16

- 150g (5½oz) rice vermicelli
- 300g (10½oz) white cabbage (about ¼ cabbage), finely shredded
- 2 carrots, grated or finely sliced into batons
- 4 tablespoons sunflower oil, plus more for frying
- 200g (7oz) mushrooms, finely chopped
- 3 spring onions, finely sliced
- 15g (½oz) coriander, stalks and leaves finely chopped, plus extra sprigs to garnish
- 16 rice paper wrappers
- 3 tablespoons sesame seeds
- salt

For the dipping sauce
(all ingredients to taste)
- 2 tablespoons soy sauce
- 1–2 teaspoons toasted sesame oil
- 1 tablespoon rice vinegar
- 1 small thumb of fresh root ginger, peeled and finely grated
- 1 garlic clove, finely grated

1. Bring a kettle to the boil and put the rice noodles in a large heatproof mixing bowl. Pour boiling water over the noodles and allow to soften for 5–7 minutes or until they are sufficiently tender. Drain and cool under cold water, then drain well again.

2. Mix your dipping sauce ingredients together, then taste and adjust if it needs more of anything. Set aside.

3. Put the cabbage and carrots in a separate mixing bowl with a good pinch of salt. Give it a good scrunch to start releasing some juice.

4. Put the oil in a pan and cook the mushrooms along with the cabbage-carrot mix over a medium heat for 2–3 minutes until it starts to wilt. Add the spring onions and coriander and cook for a further 1–2 minutes, then remove to a bowl. Once cool, mix with the rice noodles.

5. Get a large dish that will fit the rice paper wrappers and put a 5mm (¼ inch) depth of water in it. Soak a wrapper for 15–20 seconds until pliable, then remove to a chopping board. Spoon some of the mixture in the centre. Fold up the bottom edge over the filling, then the left edge, then the right. Finally, fold the top edge of the wrapper over the filling to form a squarish parcel. Repeat to fill and roll all the wrappers.

6. Set a large frying pan over a medium heat and add 1–2 tablespoons of oil. Place the sesame seeds in a bowl. Brush each parcel with a little water on the seamless side and dip into the sesame seeds. Gently fry the parcels in the pan in batches, unseeded side down first as this helps to seal the seams, until crisp and golden. Then flip and cook the sesame side until golden. Watch this carefully, as the seeds tend to catch. Don't overcrowd the pan, but you can cook many dumplings at a time – just add a litte more oil for each batch. When they're done, garnish with extra sprigs of coriander and serve with the dipping sauce.

ASSEMBLY JOBS (MOSTLY)

TOTAL TIME: **10 MINUTES**

Borlotti bean, tomato & red onion salad

A brilliant bean salad – based around ingredients from the storecupboard – for when you need something fast that both tastes great and looks good on the table. Equally, you can soak and then cook up dried borlotti (see page 82): you will need about 250g (9oz) dried weight to yield 500g (1lb 2oz) of cooked beans.

Scoop this up with flatbreads or pile it on toast and the yogurt base really brings it all together. It's equally great as a side dish. Bonus breakfast hack: save the oil from sundried tomato jars to fry eggs.

SERVES 2 AS A LIGHT MEAL, OR 4 AS A SIDE DISH

- 2 × 400g (14oz) cans of borlotti beans, drained
- 170g (6oz) jar of sundried tomatoes, drained
- 1 small red onion, finely sliced
- 2 tablespoons drained capers, chopped if large
- good pinch of dried oregano
- 3–4 tablespoons extra virgin olive oil, to taste, plus more to serve
- 2–3 tablespoons red wine vinegar, or other vinegars work fine, to taste
- 150g (5½oz) yogurt
- salt

1. Lightly rinse the canned beans. Roughly slice each sundried tomato half into 3. Add to a mixing bowl with the beans, onion and capers. Dress with the oregano, a good pinch of salt and half the oil and vinegar. Taste and add more of any ingredient you think it needs, especially for the dressing. You can leave the mixture to stand at this point, as it will only improve.

2. Spread the yogurt out on individual dishes or a serving platter. Pile on the bean mixture, add a final drizzle of olive oil and serve.

ASSEMBLY JOBS (MOSTLY)

TOTAL TIME: **40 MINUTES**

Tiger salad summer rolls with double-dunk sauce

I love Vietnamese summer rolls but these have a little twist: a zingy, fresh Chinese salad in place of the usual suspects. In Chinese, the salad is known as *lao hu cai*, which translates to 'tiger vegetable', either because the mixture looks like a tiger's stripes, or perhaps because the salad's spicy flavours impart the strength of a tiger. Be warned, you will want to overfill these and I have learned the hard way: they just burst. Fly close to the sun by all means, but satisfaction lies in a complete parcel. Feel free to add marinated and roasted batons or strips of tofu for a little protein. MAKES 16

- 150g (5½oz) rice vermicelli
- 1 cucumber, cut into 7.5cm (3 inch) batons, or to taste
- 4 celery sticks, finely sliced, or to taste
- 25g (1oz) coriander, leaves picked, stalks finely chopped, or to taste
- 1–2 green or red chillies, finely sliced, or to taste
- 1 scant tablespoon rice vinegar, or to taste
- 2 teaspoons toasted sesame oil, or to taste
- 16 rice paper wrappers
- salt

For the sauce
(all ingredients to taste)
- 75g (2¾oz) tahini
- 4 teaspoons rice vinegar
- 1½ teaspoons soy sauce
- 1 teaspoon honey
- ¾ teaspoon fine sea salt
- 100g (3½oz) roasted, salted peanuts, roughly chopped

1. Bring a kettle to the boil and put the rice noodles in a large heatproof mixing bowl. Pour boiling water over the noodles and allow to soften for 5–7 minutes or until they are sufficiently tender. Drain and cool under cold water, then drain well again.

2. Meanwhile, combine all the sauce ingredients except the peanuts in a serving bowl. Taste and add more of anything you think it needs. Put the peanuts in another bowl.

3. In a separate mixing bowl, mix the cucumber, celery, coriander and chillies and dress with the rice vinegar and sesame oil. Add a pinch of salt and any other ingredient you may think there needs to be more of.

4. Get a large dish that will fit the rice paper wrappers and put a 5mm (¼ inch) depth of water in it. Soak a wrapper for 15–20 seconds until pliable, then remove to a chopping board. Add a small handful of the noodles to the centre, spreading them in a rough horizontal line 10–12.5cm (4–5 inches) in length. Follow with the same of the tiger salad, spreading it out in the same manner. Fold the bottom edge nearest to you over the filling. Then fold in the sides over the filling, too. Finally, roll the filling up and away from you to form a neat cylinder. Repeat to fill and roll all the summer rolls.

5. Serve with the dipping sauce, using the chopped peanuts as a secondary dip for crunch.

ASSEMBLY JOBS (MOSTLY)

TOTAL TIME: **20–25 MINUTES**

Hispi fattoush

This is wonderful on its own, or as a side dish at a barbecue. Using hispi cabbage instead of lettuce makes it a bit more substantial. Also known as sweetheart or pointed spring cabbage, hispi has a mild sweet flavour that works well raw or cooked and we love them in our house. It is also fine to substitute white cabbage here, or Brussels sprouts would work, or equally – and returning to a version closer to the Lebanese original – use 2 baby gem or a good-sized romaine lettuce.

The elements can be made ahead, so this truly is pure assembly when you are ready. Cut the fresh salad ingredients and keep in a sealed container in the fridge. Make the dressing. Make the toasted pitta and keep sealed in an airtight container. Or, if you're making it when you want to eat, getting the pitta toasting while you chop the salad means it is a super-quick meal to bring together. SERVES 4

- 3 pittas, split in half, or 4 wheat tortilla wraps work, too (for homemade, see page 72)
- 1 head of hispi cabbage, shredded in roughly 2cm (¾ inch) strips
- 1 cucumber, or 2 small Persian cucumbers, cut into chunky slices
- 3 spring onions, sliced
- 250–300g (9–10½oz) cherry tomatoes, on the vine if possible, halved
- 25g (1oz) mint, leaves picked and roughly chopped
- 25g (1oz) parsley, leaves picked and roughly chopped
- 2–3 teaspoons sumac
- 10–20g (¼–¾oz) za'atar
- 6 tablespoons extra virgin olive oil, plus more for cooking and (optional) to serve
- 1 tablespoon pomegranate molasses
- finely grated zest and juice of 1 lemon, or to taste
- sea salt flakes

1. If using the oven to toast the pitta, preheat it to 220°C/200°C fan (425°F), Gas Mark 7. Or set a frying pan over a medium heat. Brush the pitta halves or tortillas with olive oil to coat evenly and sprinkle with a small amount of salt. Lay them on a couple of baking trays and cook for 15–20 minutes, turning halfway, until golden and crisp. Otherwise, toast in batches in a frying pan over a medium heat for 2 minutes on each side; I like to flip them a few times to cook evenly and you may need an extra splash of oil to stop them catching. If they are getting too dark too quickly, reduce the heat. Once crisp and golden, set aside.

2. Either break the toasted flatbread up in your hands, or chop into roughly 2cm (¾ inch) pieces; it doesn't need to be exact.

3. Meanwhile, combine the remaining ingredients in a large mixing bowl with a good pinch of sea salt flakes. Add more salt, oil or lemon zest or juice to taste. Serve.

TOTAL TIME: **15–20 MINUTES**

Bhel puri

On the way home to East London after a shoot, I used to stop off in Whitechapel, especially if I hadn't had lunch, but also just as a treat. My target was a portion of *bhel puri*, either from a hole-in-the-wall kiosk I had been tipped off about, or the bloke with a cart outside the mosque. I've made this version a bit more substantial with a boosted amount of chickpeas, so you can cut back on those for a snack version. Either way, this is a great early-summer-onwards meal that is ready in no time.

If you have time, you can soak and then cook up dried chickpeas (see page 82 or 200): you will need about 125g (4½oz) dried weight to yield 250g (9oz) of cooked chickpeas.

Try using carlin peas instead of chickpeas, or puffed quinoa in place of rice. I use packets of Hodmedods roasted beans and peas, as I enjoy the extra layer of flavour and texture they bring, plus they aren't fried. I know it strays from the traditional, but I like this version and always keep the dry elements in stock so that the dish can be assembled with just a couple of extra bits. SERVES 4

- 60g (2¼oz) puffed brown rice
- 400g (14oz) can of chickpeas, drained
- 250g (9oz) tomatoes, chopped
- 1 cucumber, chopped
- 1 small red onion, finely chopped
- 1 green chilli, finely chopped, or more if you like
- 60g (2¼oz) roasted peanuts, lightly crushed
- 125g (4½oz) roasted fava beans or roasted peas, or fine sev (crunchy chickpea noodles), or good-quality Bombay mix at a pinch
- 25g (1oz) coriander, leaves roughly chopped, stalks finely chopped
- lime quarters, to serve

For the tamarind sauce
- finely grated zest and juice of 2 limes
- 1 thumb of fresh root ginger, peeled and finely chopped or finely grated
- 3 tablespoons tamarind paste
- 1–2 teaspoons chaat masala, or good-quality curry powder

1. Start with the tamarind sauce. In a small bowl, mix the lime zest and juice with the ginger, tamarind and chaat masala or curry powder, adding a tablespoon or so of water to loosen: you want it runny enough to coat, but not too watery.

2. Mix all the remaining ingredients in a mixing bowl, except the roasted beans or peas or sev and a pinch of the coriander leaves. Toss the sauce over. Divide between plates or arrange on a serving platter.

3. Top with the roasted beans or peas or sev and reserved coriander leaves and serve with lime quarters for squeezing over.

TOTAL TIME: **15–20 MINUTES**

Silken tofu bun xa

A streamlined midweek dinner you can serve without putting the oven on, and if you use silken tofu in a Tetra Pak, it's shelf-stable, ready and waiting for you to make this dish. If you don't like how silken tofu breaks up, go with a firmer variety, but warm it through in a pan of seasoned warm water gently, as that massively improves the texture. By all means, use the Crispy Tofu from page 159 here instead if you like; it is wonderful, but does involve the oven. Lemongrass keeps really well in the freezer if you aren't going to use it all, or want it always on hand.

I love to pile up all the individual elements here on a large baking tray or serving platter, then put it in the middle of the table for everyone to help themselves. This way of serving is particularly popular with children or fussy eaters (see pages 118–19). SERVES 4

- 2 lemongrass stalks (optional), crushed with the side of a knife
- 200g (7oz) rice vermicelli
- 1 baby gem lettuce, shredded
- ½ cucumber, thinly sliced or cut into batons
- 2 small carrots, grated or julienned
- 2 spring onions, sliced
- 2 × 300g (10½oz) blocks of silken tofu, liberated of packaging, each cut into 8 slices
- 15g (½oz) coriander, roughly chopped
- 15g (½oz) mint, leaves picked
- 4 tablespoons crushed roasted peanuts (both unsalted and salted work fine)

For the dressing
- 3 tablespoons rice vinegar
- juice of 2 limes
- 2 lemongrass stalks, tough outer layers removed, soft cores finely chopped
- 1 red chilli, finely chopped
- 1–2 teaspoons sugar, or honey
- 2 teaspoons soy sauce, or a good pinch of salt
- 1 garlic clove, thinly sliced

1. Bring a saucepan of water to the boil with the lemongrass stalks inside. Remove from the heat, add the noodles and allow to soften in the lemongrass-infused water for 5–7 minutes or until they are sufficiently tender. Drain the noodles either directly into bowls, or cool under cold water if you want the dish to be more refreshing, then drain well again.

2. Meanwhile, mix together the dressing ingredients, then taste and adjust the balance of sweet and sour accordingly. Set aside.

3. Divide the noodles between bowls. Top with little piles of each veg. Add the tofu and herbs and sprinkle with the peanuts, then pour the dressing over everything to serve.

ASSEMBLY JOBS (MOSTLY)

TOTAL TIME: **25-30 MINUTES**

Buffalo chickpea crunch wrap

This chickpea mixture is equally great as a salad (good for a packed lunch) or a wrap. If you're making it as a salad to take with you, pack the tomatoes and lettuce separately and mix them in when you come to eat. The ratios align perfectly with my tastes, but please have a play and swap in or increase items to suit yours. I use pre-cooked chickpeas here but if you like you can soak and then cook up some dried chickpeas (see page 82 or 200): you will need about 250g (9oz) dried weight to yield 500g (1lb 2oz) of cooked chickpeas.
SERVES 4

- 2 × 400g (14oz) cans of chickpeas, drained
- 4 tablespoons hot sauce (for homemade, see page 75), plus more (optional) to serve
- 1 teaspoon garlic powder, or 1 garlic clove, finely grated
- 1 celery stick, finely chopped
- 1 small red onion, finely chopped, or 2 spring onions, finely sliced
- 4 flatbreads (larger breads make your folding life easier)
- 125g (4½oz) blue cheese, crumbled
- 100g (3½oz) cherry tomatoes, roughly quartered
- 1 baby gem, or ½ romaine lettuce, shredded
- flavourless oil, for cooking
- salt

For the tahini sauce
- 75g (2¾oz) tahini
- finely grated zest and juice of 1 lemon
- 75ml (2½fl oz) cold water

1. For the sauce, whisk the tahini with the lemon zest and juice and a good pinch of salt. Add enough of the measured water to loosen the mixture and form a sauce; fluid but not runny is the key.

2. Toss the chickpeas in a mixing bowl with the hot sauce and garlic, gently crushing a few chickpeas to help the mixture come together. Stir through the celery and onion. Taste and adjust the seasoning.

3. Gently warm the flatbreads in a dry frying pan, just to make them malleable. Or – if you keep an eye on them – I turn the toaster on and warm them laid over the top. Be careful they don't catch and burn; they only need a light heat.

4. Spread some tahini sauce on the flatbreads. Pile the chickpea mixture into the centres, then the cheese, tomatoes and lettuce. With the wrap in front of you, fold up the edge closest to you. Then, moving right, fold the next section of wrap into the middle. Then the next one round. Repeat 2 more times until you have a neat pentagon. You can try for a hexagon, but I always run out of foldable sides.

5. Brush a tiny bit of oil over a frying pan and toast the wraps on each side – starting with the seam side, as it helps seal the wrap – until golden and crisp. Go slowly, as you want the cheese to melt and the filling to be warm right through. Enjoy with extra hot sauce, if you like.

ASSEMBLY JOBS (MOSTLY)

TOTAL TIME: **5–10 MINUTES**

Tofu with broken rice paper & spicy sauce

I first made this dish when I needed to rush out the door but have a quick lunch before I did. I wanted something that wouldn't be too heavy, and ready in pretty much five minutes. I didn't have noodles, but figured the already-starting-to-break rice paper wrappers at the back of the cupboard could be helped on their way to being a base for tofu and a spicy sauce. The 'noodles' are cold from the water, the tofu at room temperature and the sauce still warm from the heated oil. A really lovely plate to eat. Add steamed or fried veg for a more substantial offering. SERVES 2

- 140g (5oz) rice paper wrappers
- 3 tablespoons sunflower oil (groundnut is also fine)
- 1–2 tablespoons rice vinegar
- 1 garlic clove, finely grated, or 1 teaspoon garlic powder
- ½ teaspoon ground turmeric
- 1 heaped teaspoon cumin seeds, crushed
- 1 tablespoon chilli flakes
- 1 tablespoon black sesame seeds (or mixed or white sesame are also fine)
- 3 tablespoons soy sauce
- 400g (14oz) silken tofu
- salt (optional)
- herb leaves, such as mint or parsley, or thinly sliced spring onion, or cucumber, to serve

1. Roughly crush up the rice paper wrappers in the packet, then pour the contents into a mixing bowl and cover with cold water. Set aside to soften.

2. Meanwhile, heat up the oil in a small saucepan until just starting to get hazy over the top. At the same time, add the remaining ingredients except the soy and tofu to a heatproof mixing bowl. Pour over the hot oil carefully and stir the mixture to get the oil in contact with all the ingredients. Add the soy. Check the seasoning and add any element you think is lacking, as well as salt if needed.

3. Check the rice wrappers are soft. If so, drain well and divide between 2 plates.

4. Drain and slice the tofu into 8 slices. Place 4 on each plate. Top with the sauce and any herbs, spring onion or cucumber you are using.

ASSEMBLY JOBS (MOSTLY)

TOTAL TIME: **30 MINUTES**

Refried bean burritos

These are based on breakfast burritos, but I never really have enough time to make them in the mornings, so I have them later on in the day instead. The name of the game here is to not overfill. I know it's tempting – the exhilarating rush you get from packing in the most amount of filling possible – but they will split, so less is more in this case. The bigger, ultimately more satisfying picture is a crunchy exterior with everything nicely packed together.

Preparation is your friend here. If you are strapped for time, or just want an easy ride at the time of making, make sure you have leftover potato around. Even the eggs can be whisked and kept in the fridge. Add rice for a more substantial option, or take the burritos up a notch by using leftover Refried Carlin Peas (see page 200) instead of the canned black beans. MAKES 4

- flavourless oil, for cooking
- 1 onion, chopped
- 1 teaspoon ground cumin
- 1 teaspoon ground coriander
- 3 garlic cloves, sliced
- 400g (14oz) can of black beans
- 4 eggs, lightly beaten
- 300g (10½oz) cold cooked potato, coarsely grated, riced, mashed or roughly chopped
- 4 large flour tortillas (for homemade, see page 72)
- 100–150g (3½–5½oz) Cheddar cheese, coarsely grated
- a few coriander leaves (optional)
- salt
- hot sauce, to serve (for homemade, see page 75)

1. Put 1–2 tablespoons of oil in a saucepan set over a medium heat and add the onion with a pinch of salt. Cook for 7–10 minutes until soft and translucent. Then add the spices and garlic and cook for a minute more. Now add the black beans with the juice from the can. Cook for 5–7 minutes until reduced and the majority of the liquid has gone. Turn off the heat and gently crush the beans with a masher, just to help them bind, leaving some whole beans.

2. Set a large frying pan over a medium heat, then add 1–2 tablespoons of oil. Quickly scramble the eggs with a good pinch of salt. Remove to a plate. Add some more oil to the same pan, followed by the grated potato. Fry until golden and crispy; 6–8 minutes should do, flipping halfway. Tip on to a plate.

3. To assemble, heat each tortilla in the frying pan gently for 30 seconds on each side. Then divide the filling ingredients – beans, eggs, potato, cheese and coriander, if using – between each. Lift the bottom side over the filling, folding the 2 sides in. Firmly tuck in the filling while you roll the wrap away from you to form a burrito. Rest it on its seam edge side. Reduce the heat of the pan to medium–low and add the burritos 2 at a time to the frying pan to toast the tortilla, seam sides down, for 1–2 minutes on each side, rotating every minute or so, until crisp. Serve with your favourite hot sauce.

ASSEMBLY JOBS (MOSTLY)

YOUR STORECUPBOARD ESSENTIALS

Many of the weeknight dishes in this chapter are really just a matter of putting agreeable elements together, alongside a little light cooking. However, in order to make such assembly-job cooking work for you on a weeknight, you will need to treat your storecupboard as your personal arsenal. This way of organizing events will come to be a state of mind in time. Until then, here is what you will need.

OIL I do love a fancy super-peppery extra virgin olive oil to finish dishes – I could pretty much drink the stuff straight from the bottle – so I try to keep a favourite bottle on hand. But I mainly use a lesser olive oil for cooking, with a good-quality sunflower oil doing the heavy lifting. For instance, I make mayonnaise mainly with sunflower oil and sometimes finish it with a little extra virgin olive oil, for flavour.

VINEGAR You can get away with a trusty do-it-all bottle, so I urge you to do so once you find a vinegar that holds a special place in your heart. But, really, the more the merrier. As with oil, I have one to cook with, then another to season, keeping a fancy bursting-with-flavour vinegar – generally sherry or other wine vinegar – to finish and dress dishes. I also keep the vinegar from jars of pickles and use it for seasoning soups or mayonnaises, or anywhere else I might need it, though remember that this might be watered down a little from its time with the veg.

PEPPER A spice that I adore and probably the only one I keep in a few different types. I have three pepper mills on the go at most times, as I really enjoy reaching for a specific pepper to add the note I'm after. One contains a great standard black pepper. The second may have another variety of black pepper, or a blend of different peppercorns. The last may house pink peppercorns, or particularly spicy peppercorns.

SALT Herb salt for finishing; sea salt flakes for finishing or more gentle seasoning; fine sea salt for cooking.

PICKLES & FERMENTS That vinegary pop of crunch and flavour adds such a lovely top note, especially to soups and stews that may need a little lift, and I keep an ever-evolving stock of pickles and ferments for brightening up winter food with their memories of sunnier days. I like to have cornichons and their large cousins, gherkins, always to hand, as well as pickled red and white onion, pickled red cabbage (see page 110), a firm favourite these days, along with carrot and daikon pickle for sandwiches, salads or stews. There are always pickled chillies, to be eaten whole, or sliced and added to salads or blended into hot sauce if they ferment (see page 75). There will be sliced cucumber quick pickles in summer and there is always sauerkraut. Pickles and ferments can also be sliced or finely diced into sauces or mayonnaises to help layer flavours.

SPICES I try not to have a massive stockpile of spices. Or, if I do get a spice in specially, I try to use it up over the coming weeks while it's at its peak. I used to pride myself on having all the spices, but many were forgotten at the back of the cupboard and were flavourless dust upon resurfacing. So these days, I favour spice blends, sometimes boosting their key elements, above making them from scratch. For instance, I'll buy a really solid medium curry powder, which on its own is a great starting place. Depending on what I am making, I might add a teaspoon of crushed fennel seeds and/or a touch of freshly crushed cumin seeds. Whatever flavour I want to stand out, I'll help prop up. This way, I have a handful of spice jars rather than a full army. It helps keep things in check. That said, I try to keep in:

- a solid sweet paprika
- bright red fresh-flavoured chilli flakes
- good-quality dried oregano
- cumin, seeds or ground
- coriander, seeds or ground
- fennel seeds
- dried mint
- za'atar
- sumac
- ground turmeric

GARLIC & ONION POWDER These have become staples. I find garlic powder doesn't give me indigestion like raw garlic does nowadays. Both garlic and onion powders go into dressings, or creamy yogurt- or mayonnaise-based sauces, as well as into dry rubs, or are added to seasoned flour before using it as a coating. They also go into batters or bread mixes to add extra flavour.

ASSEMBLY JOBS (MOSTLY)

MIX & MAKE

We are stepping up a gear here with dishes that are rather heartier for when you want something warming and, dare I say it, a bit more comforting while still being light on their feet. You will find reimagined favourites like fail-safe bean burgers, fast falafel and supersized croquettes, along with ready-filled homemade flatbreads for the perfectly portable lunch or snack on the go.

TOTAL TIME: 30 MINUTES

Brothy butter beans with steamed dumplings

Feeling a little cold? Craving cosy comfort? Look no further! This is satisfyingly straightforward to make and guaranteed to be a big hug in a bowl. While warming and great served in front of a roaring fire, I do also rather like this on those spring or autumn days when you can just about eat outside. It helps bridge the gaps between the seasons and their fluctuating temperatures. Anyway, this is very pleasing to eat at pretty much any time of year.
SERVES 4

- 2 tablespoons flavourless oil
- 2 onions, roughly chopped
- 3 celery sticks, sliced
- 3 garlic cloves, sliced
- 200–300g (7–10½oz) chard, stalks finely chopped, leaves roughly chopped, kept separate
- 2 × 400g (14oz) cans of butter beans, drained
- 500ml (18fl oz) hot vegetable stock
- salt and black pepper
- olive oil, to serve

For the dumplings
- 200g (7oz) flour (I use white spelt, but most will work well)
- 1 teaspoon baking powder
- 25g (1oz) dill, finely chopped
- 200g (7oz) yogurt, or kefir
- salt

1. Set a saucepan that will both fit everything – including the dumplings after they have expanded – and has a lid over a medium heat and add the flavourless oil. Follow with the onions and celery with a pinch of salt. Cook for 10–12 minutes until softened. Then follow with the garlic, chard stalks, beans and stock. Simmer gently while you make the dumplings.

2. Mix the flour with the baking powder, a pinch of salt and the dill in a mixing bowl. Add the yogurt or kefir and incorporate fully to form a dough.

3. Stir the chard leaves into the beans.

4. Wet your hands and shape the dough into 12 walnut-sized dumplings, then add them to the brothy beans. Once they are all in, cover the pan with the lid. Bubble away over a medium/medium–low heat for 10–12 minutes. If you are unsure whether the dumplings are cooked, take one out and break it open to ensure it is cooked through with no trace of wet dough inside. Serve with a drizzle of olive oil.

TOTAL TIME: 45 MINUTES – 1 HOUR

Pea & potato pancakes with two chutneys

These green pancakes are really fresh-tasting with such a wonderful, vibrant pea flavour. Teamed with potato curry, they are a delight.

These are, of course, based on dosas, but are a much speedier offering. MAKES ABOUT 12

1. Blitz the split peas in a blender or spice grinder. Then add in the measured water, continuing to blend to a smooth batter, with the eggs, coriander, chilli, if using, ginger and oil.

2. For the chutneys, divide the coconut and ginger between 2 small mixing bowls. To one, add the tomato purée, chilli powder and 100ml (3½fl oz) of the measured warm water. Mix, add a pinch of salt and set aside. To the other bowl, add the lemon juice, chilli, cumin, coriander and remaining measured warm water. Mix, add a pinch of salt and set aside.

3. For the filling, heat the oil in a pan. Add the mustard seeds and cook for 30 seconds, then follow with the potatoes, curry powder and chilli powder, if using. Add enough water to just cover, bring to a simmer and cook for 8 minutes. Add the cabbage and cook for a further 2–7 minutes until the potato is fully cooked through and the water has completely gone, topping up with a little water at a time if needed. Check the seasoning and add salt if needed.

4. Over a medium heat, warm up a 24cm (9½ inch) frying pan. Add a splash of oil and pour in some of the pea batter. It should be fluid enough to be rolled around the pan to fill out to the edges. If not, blend in a little more water. Cook gently for 2–3 minutes until set. Carefully flip over and cook for a further minute. Flip the pancake back over and remove to a plate. Add some potato curry, rolling the pancake over the filling and serve with the chutneys alongside. Repeat to cook and fill the remaining pancakes.

For the pancakes
- 250g (9oz) green split peas
- 300ml (½ pint) water
- 4 eggs
- 25g (1oz) coriander
- 1–2 green chillies (optional)
- ½ small thumb of fresh root ginger, peeled
- 2 tablespoons flavourless oil (I use sunflower oil), plus more for cooking

For the two chutneys
- 120g (4¼oz) coconut flakes, blitzed in a blender or small food processor, or desiccated coconut
- 4cm (1½ inch) piece of fresh root ginger, peeled and finely grated
- 2 tablespoons tomato purée
- ½–1 teaspoon Kashmiri chilli powder
- 175ml (6fl oz) warm water
- juice of 1 lemon
- 1 green chilli, finely chopped
- 1 teaspoon ground cumin
- 7g (¼oz) coriander, finely chopped
- salt

For the filling
- 2 tablespoons flavourless oil
- 1 tablespoon brown mustard seeds
- 400g (14oz) potatoes, scrubbed and cut into 1cm (½ inch) cubes
- 1 tablespoon curry powder
- 1 teaspoon Kashmiri chilli powder (optional)
- 200g (7oz) white cabbage, shredded
- salt, if needed

MIX & MAKE

TOTAL TIME: 30–35 MINUTES

'Stir-fry' fridge fritters

I've lost count of the number of times I've made these; they are a go-to staple, stretching odds and ends of veg into a full meal. As well as welcoming spice or herb additions, they marry happily with most things you throw in them. If you like, you can use beaten eggs to bind the mixture instead of water. I like to spread the mixture out when spooning into the pan to make an American pancake-type shape (these will cook through more quickly). I call these 'stir-fry' fritters, as the veg that tends to get included always reminds me of the stir-fry I used to be made as a child. MAKES 12

- 200g (7oz) gram (chickpea) flour
- 1 tablespoon baking powder
- 200ml (7fl oz) water, plus more if needed
- 1 large onion, or 2 medium onions, finely sliced
- 500g (1lb 2oz) veg, such as cabbage, peppers, carrots, fennel, greens, and spring onions, shredded
- 25g (1oz) soft herbs, such as mint, dill, parsley or coriander (a mixture to use up odds and ends is fine), finely chopped
- 2 tablespoons flavourless oil (I use sunflower), plus more for cooking
- salt
- yogurt or crème fraîche, to serve

1. In a mixing bowl, mix the flour with the baking powder, then stir in the measured water and a good pinch of salt. Fold in the veg, herbs and oil. Add more water if you think it needs it, but the batter is mostly just to coat the veg.

2. Heat a large frying pan or flat griddle over a medium–low heat. Add some oil for cooking and spoon some of the mixture into piles that don't crowd the pan. Cook for 3–4 minutes on each side until cooked through and puffed in the middle. Remove from the pan and continue to cook the remaining mixture.

3. Serve with yogurt or crème fraîche.

TOTAL: **50 MINUTES – 1 HOUR**

Griddled olive, tomato & basil flatbreads

Everyone in my family is a fan of bread studded with salty briny olives, and this recipe just takes that craving a step further. Feel free to take an even further step by adding a block of grated halloumi to the mix; these flatbreads really are a springboard for you to have a play.

As these are great for knocking up quickly, I batch-make them, cut them in half and freeze them. When I want one, I pop it in the toaster to defrost and crisp from frozen.

Also try using them as a wrap for gyros. MAKES 4

- 400g (14oz) self-raising flour, or plain flour with 1 tablespoon baking powder
- 200g (7oz) wholemeal flour, plus more to dust
- 250g (9oz) yogurt, or kefir
- 3 tablespoons olive oil, or oil from the sundried tomatoes, plus more (optional) for cooking
- 200ml (7fl oz) water
- 200g (7oz) jar of sundried tomatoes in olive oil, drained and sliced
- 50g (1¾oz) black olives, pitted and sliced
- 25g (1oz) basil, stalks finely chopped, leaves chopped
- 3 tablespoon drained capers
- 1 tablespoon dried oregano

To serve (all optional)
- pesto
- harissa
- tapenade
- pickled chillies

1. Put the flours in a mixing bowl. Mix the yogurt or kefir in a jug with the oil and measured water. Add to the flour and knead to combine. Knead in the sundried tomatoes, olives, basil, capers and oregano.

2. Divide the dough into 4 and roll out each piece on a floured surface to a diameter of about 20cm (8 inches).

3. Heat a griddle pan over a medium–low heat. Add the flatbreads one at a time, brushing with olive oil first to get them extra-crispy, if you like. Cook for 4–6 minutes on each side until puffed and cooked through. If worried about whether they're ready, break a chunk off one, pull it apart and see if it is fluffy in the middle.

4. Serve as is, or on the side of a meal, or spread with pesto, harissa or tapenade, or with a bowl of pickled chillies.

TOTAL TIME: 35–45 MINUTES, PLUS RESTING AND PROVING

Malthouse muffins

These are often requested for breakfast in our house and they do make a cracking option with a folded omelette with cheese melting in the middle, sliced avocado and hot sauce. Or try simply sliced in half, buttered and topped however you please.

I like to mix the dough in the evening, portion the divided dough balls into oiled round containers about 500ml (18fl oz) in capacity, stack them in the fridge to prove overnight, then in the morning simply turn out and cook. (The best non-plastic containers I have found are metal tiffin tins.) The dough can stay proving for up to 48 hours in the fridge. Make and shape the dough when you have a moment, then cook as needed.

The pasta flour here makes muffins that cook fairly quickly, while the malthouse flour adds interest. By all means, have a play with different ratios: all white flour works, as does all malthouse, however with the latter you may need around 100ml (3½fl oz) more water. MAKES 10–12 SMALLISH MUFFINS

- 450g (1lb) 00 flour, or pasta flour
- 150g (5½oz) malthouse flour
- 15g (½oz) fine sea salt
- 5g (1/8oz) fast-action dried yeast
- 400ml (14fl oz) chilled water
- flavourless oil, for greasing
- 200g (7oz) semolina, or polenta (or more flour also works)

1. Put all the dry ingredients except the semolina or polenta in a mixing bowl, or a stand mixer fitted with a dough hook, then pour in 250ml (9fl oz) of the chilled water. If making by hand, mix with your hand until the dough starts to come together, then knead in the bowl while gradually splashing in the remaining water. If making in a stand mixer, start the machine on low to combine everything. Then increase the speed to high and add the remaining water a trickle at a time until fully incorporated. This should take 5–10 minutes.

2. Remove the dough and shape into a ball on a work surface by tucking the edges underneath and into the centre. Upturn the mixing or mixer bowl over the dough and allow to rest for 15–30 minutes.

3. Oil individual containers well or, if cooking straight away, a large baking sheet. Divide the dough, either by eye or by weighing each piece, into 10–12 near-enough equal parts. With each, repeat the folding in the edges underneath to the centre as before. Place in the containers, put the lid on and place in the fridge overnight. Or space out on the large baking sheet and leave to prove for 45 minutes – 1 hour.

4. If your muffins are in the fridge, remove them and allow them to come to room temperature 30 minutes – 1 hour before you want to cook them, if you have time. When ready, heat a heavy-based frying pan or cast-iron pan over a medium–low heat. Tip the semolina or polenta into a mixing bowl. Gently turn out each muffin, one at a time, into the semolina or polenta. Flip to coat all over.

5. Place the muffins in the pan and cook in batches until risen and golden on the bottom; 6–9 minutes. Flip and repeat on the other side until risen and cooked through, flipping back and forth so that they don't overcook on one side, until done. If you have a probe thermometer, the temperature in the centre of the cooked muffins should be 93°C (199°F) or above.

TOTAL TIME: **55 MINUTES**

Chard & Cheddar galettes

I've always been drawn to savoury galettes – they're such a wonderful vehicle to stuff with your favourite seasonal veg. You can crack the eggs into the middle of the folded galettes and bake them in the oven until done, if you prefer, but I like the boiling-and-cutting method, as they look good and it speeds things up a bit. Swap in any other greens you have: baby spinach, kale, cavolo nero, even broccoli. As for the cheese, if you are using a milder variety, you may need more of it. Equally, go big on the cheese anyway, grating some over the folded galettes and baking or grilling in the oven until melted and golden. MAKES 4 LARGE GALETTES

- 100g (3½oz) buckwheat flour
- 300ml (½ pint) whole milk
- 9 eggs
- 1 tablespoon flavourless oil, plus more for cooking
- 1 onion, finely chopped
- 200g (7oz) mushrooms, torn or finely chopped
- 400g (14oz) chard, leaves stripped and torn, stalks finely chopped
- 1–2 tablespoons Dijon mustard
- 150g (5½oz) mature Cheddar cheese, or another cheese you like, grated
- 15g (½oz) mix of herb leaves, such as parsley, dill, chervil and chopped chives (optional)
- salt and black pepper
- 4 tablespoons crème fraîche, to serve (optional)

1. Either in a mixing bowl with a whisk or in a blender, combine the flour, milk and 5 of the eggs with a good pinch of salt. Add the oil and whisk or blend until smooth. Set aside.

2. Put the remaining 4 eggs in a saucepan and cover with water. Bring gently to a simmer. Allow to bubble away for 3 minutes, then turn off the heat, cover the pan and leave to stand for 5 minutes. Remove and shell the eggs under running cold water. Set aside.

3. Put 2 tablespoons of oil in a large frying pan (I use a 30cm/12 inch one). Add the onion with a pinch of salt and cook until translucent; 10–12 minutes. Now add the mushrooms and chard stalks and cook for a further 3–5 minutes until softened. Add the leaves and cook for a further 2 minutes until wilted. Taste and season with salt and pepper. Remove from the pan and set aside.

4. Wipe out the pan. Add a splash of oil and heat over a medium-low heat. Add one-quarter of the batter, roll the pan to evenly disperse the batter and cook gently for 1–2 minutes until just set. Brush with mustard. Add one-quarter of the cheese evenly, then spoon in one-quarter of the greens mix. In the pan, fold in the sides of the galette: either 4 to make a square, or 3 for a triangle. Remove to a plate. Cut a boiled egg in half, place in the middle and garnish with black pepper. Scatter with herbs and serve with crème fraîche, if you like. Repeat to cook and fill the remaining galettes. You can make these to the filled-and-folded stage and keep them warm in a low oven, if you want to serve them all at once.

MIX & MAKE

TOTAL TIME: **45 MINUTES**

Best-behaved black bean burgers

I wanted a burger that was good to eat, didn't just crumble after the first bite and that satisfied non-vegetarians. This does all three, according to the feedback! I also wanted it to be as easy to cook as possible, and handle well in the pan or on the grill. I often shape these into squares if we don't have buns in the house, so that they fit well between slices of bread. The burgers are happy to be made ahead and sit waiting in the fridge, but aren't any bother just to roll on through and make to completion either. MAKES 8

- 100g (3½oz) dried quinoa
- 2 tablespoons flavourless oil, plus more for cooking
- 1 onion, finely chopped
- 200g (7oz) chestnut, portobello or button mushrooms, finely chopped
- 2 garlic cloves, crushed or finely grated
- 1 teaspoon smoked paprika
- 1 teaspoon ground cumin
- 100g (3½oz) ground linseed
- 100ml (3½fl oz) water
- 2 × 400g (14oz) cans of black beans, drained well and patted dry
- 15g (½oz) cornflour
- salt and black pepper

To serve (all optional)
- toasted buns or bread slices
- sliced onion, raw or cooked
- sliced tomatoes
- lettuce
- sliced gherkins
- cheese slices
- tomato sauce

1. Cook the quinoa in a saucepan of water with a pinch of salt until collapsing; you will most likely want to cook it for 1½ times what it says on the packet. Drain well and spread out on a tray to allow the steam to release. This bit is quite important.

2. Meanwhile, in a separate saucepan, heat the oil and cook the onion over a medium–low heat for 8–12 minutes until soft and translucent. Add the mushrooms and continue cooking for a further 8–10 minutes until all the moisture has gone. Stir in the garlic and cook for 1–2 minutes. Add the paprika and cumin, cook for a minute more, then turn off the heat.

3. Mix the linseed with the measured water in a bowl and set aside to form a paste.

4. Crush the black beans with a masher to break some of them down; texture is good here, but enough should be crushed so that they bind together. Stir in the quinoa, the onion and mushrooms, the linseed mixture and the cornflour, and season well with salt and pepper.

5. Form into 8 patties. These can be made ahead, covered and left in the fridge for a day or so. Or just roll straight on with cooking in oil in a frying pan or on a barbecue for 3–5 minutes on each side over a medium heat, flipping a couple of times. Assemble the burgers however you prefer and tuck in.

TOTAL TIME: **15 MINUTES**

Tomato-fennel pasta with rocket salad

This was originally a vodka pasta sauce, but it's now evolved to be a bit extra. My son's favourite veg is fennel, so that naturally found its way in, and the vodka has been swapped for wine, as the flavour addition is welcome. Dumping a load of peppery rocket on top helps cut the richness. I like the square shape of *spaghetti alla chitarra*, and I recommend that you seek it out if you haven't discovered it yet. SERVES 4

- 400g (14oz) spaghetti (see recipe introduction), or other pasta shapes work well
- 2 small fennel bulbs
- 2 tablespoons olive oil
- 3 garlic cloves, finely sliced
- 200g (7oz) tomato purée (I use a jar of the Biona brand)
- 150ml (¼ pint) white wine (or cider works well, too)
- 100g (3½oz) crème fraîche
- 150g (5½oz) rocket
- juice of 1 lemon
- 50g (1¾oz) hard cheese, such as Spenwood, shaved with a vegetable peeler or crumbled
- 2 tablespoons extra virgin olive oil
- sea salt flakes and black pepper

1. Bring a large pan of well-salted water to the boil. Add the pasta to the water, aiming to cook it for a minute less than stated on the packet instructions.

2. Meanwhile, trim the tough woody stalks from the fennel bulbs, then cut them in half and lay them on a work surface, cut side down, with the root facing you. Now slice them root to tip.

3. Put the olive oil in a large frying pan over a medium heat and follow with the fennel. Cook for 3–4 minutes until wilted, adding the garlic for the last minute. Add the tomato purée along with the wine. Bring to a simmer and stir to incorporate any lumps, then add the crème fraîche and reduce the heat to the lowest setting to keep it all warm.

4. Mix the rocket, lemon juice, hard cheese and extra virgin olive oil in a bowl with salt and pepper to taste.

5. When the pasta is done, drain, reserving a cup of the pasta cooking water, and add to the fennel and tomato pan, stirring and splashing in the water as needed to make a silky sauce. Serve on plates or in bowls, topped with the salad.

TOTAL TIME: 35–45 MINUTES

Potato-stuffed flatbreads

These are a template that can take most flavours you throw at them, such as cooked greens, different spices, loads of herbs... pretty much anything you can think of. Years ago, when I was working as a photography assistant in Hoxton, on rare occasions we reached lunchtime and didn't have anything made to eat, or even ingredients to use. We were so used to photographing food that the fridge was usually full to bursting, and on those occasions when we weren't, nobody thought to fill it. So we'd pop round the corner and get a selection of *gözleme*, stuffed with potato and chilli, potato and cheese or potato and spinach, along with a few tubs of hummus to dip them in and a leafy salad.

You can roll these out so they are thinner – similar to *gözleme* – and then cook, or equally leave them more compact, depending on your mood. Add cooked chickpeas or other pulses to the filling to make a more substantial offering. They are great for packed lunches and a good reason to make more crushed or mashed potato than you need, just for the leftovers. MAKES 8

- 1 onion, finely chopped
- 3 tablespoons oil (olive or sunflower work well), plus more for cooking
- 350–400g (12–14oz) yogurt
- 400g (14oz) self-raising flour, or plain flour with 1 tablespoon baking powder, plus more to dust
- 500g (1lb 2oz) cold cooked potato (crushed or mashed works)
- 1–2 green chillies, finely chopped
- salt

1. Set a frying pan over a medium heat with a splash of oil, then cook the onion until translucent. Set aside.

2. Mix a good pinch of salt with the oil, yogurt and flour in a large mixing bowl. Bring it together and knead gently so that it is smooth and no dry bits of flour are left; a couple of minutes is more than enough. Divide into 8 balls.

3. Mix the potato, onion and chilli together. On a floured surface, roll out a ball of dough to about 12cm (4½ inches) in diameter. Spoon on a portion (about one-eighth) of the potato mix. Grab an edge of the dough and pull it into the middle. Repeat this all the way around and pinch together in the centre to completely encase the filling. Flip them over and give them a gentle pat down. They should be around 8cm (3¼ inches) in diameter. However, if you want to roll them out thinner, dust them lightly with flour and gently – with single-direction strokes of a rolling pin – take them as thin as you dare. If the dough splits, just stop there and cook them as they are; it isn't too much of a big deal. Whichever way you do it, repeat to stuff and form all 8 breads.

4. In a large frying pan or on a flat griddle, cook the flatbreads over a medium–low heat for 4–6 minutes on each side until golden and crisp. You will probably have to do this in 2 batches, depending on the size of your pan. Serve warm alongside other dishes, or take with you to enjoy at room temperature as a packed lunch.

TOTAL TIME: **45–55 MINUTES**

Whipped tofu with charred broccoli & red onion

The trick here is to use firm tofu and blend it well until smooth. Silken tofu will leach out its water and, anyway, doesn't have the presence required here. You can also just make the whipped tofu and use it elsewhere: it is excellent on toast with blistered tomatoes. Just as it does here, it adds a cooling creaminess that ties everything together. I tend to use a pre-made good-quality rub or spice blend, but if you don't, just use what you have, such as paprika, garlic powder or grated garlic, ground cumin, ground coriander, toasted and ground fennel seeds... anything that would work well in a barbecue rub, in other words. SERVES 4

- 700g (1lb 9oz) broccoli
- 3–4 tablespoons flavourless oil
- 3 red onions, quartered from top to bottom, or thickly sliced
- 2–3 tablespoons spice mix, such as a smoky barbecue rub, or ras el hanout (or see recipe introduction)
- couple of handfuls of soft herb leaves, such as mint, dill, parsley or coriander (optional)
- salt

For the whipped tofu
- 450g (1lb) firm tofu, drained
- 100ml (3½fl oz) water
- 2 tablespoons extra virgin olive oil, plus more to serve

1. Preheat the oven to 230°C/210°C fan (450°F), Gas Mark 8. Trim the end 1cm (½ inch) or so off the heads of broccoli. Break off the florets, then slice the stalks into 1–2cm (½–¾ inch) sections; it's quite fun to have some cross-sections of the whole head of broccoli, too. Place in a bowl, toss with the oil and red onions and add a good pinch of salt, then lay out on a large baking tray, or use 2 if it looks a bit crowded. Roast for 25 minutes. Remove from the oven and flip everything over, then return to the oven and cook until cooked through and with caramelized edges; another 15–25 minutes. With 5 minutes to go, sprinkle in the spice mix.

2. Meanwhile, to make the whipped tofu, put the tofu in a blender or food processor (I think a blender does a better job here) with the measured water and a generous pinch of salt. Blend until silky-smooth; you will need to scrape down the sides to help incorporate everything. Add a small trickle of water to get it moving well to a super-smooth sauce: too much and it will be too thin, so just add a tiny amount each time.

3. Spread out the tofu on a serving platter or plates. Pile on the broccoli and red onion mixture. Scatter with the herbs, if using, and drizzle with extra virgin olive oil, to serve.

MIX & MAKE

TOTAL TIME: **15 MINUTES**

Ajo blanco
(sauce or soup)

I first came across the Andalusian soup *ajo blanco* used as a sauce when working with Laura Jackson at Towpath Café on the Regent's Canal in London. Like all the best ideas, once someone has it, it seems such an obvious thing to do.

You can make it the consistency of mayonnaise and use it in place of that, but be warned, it is very dangerous. You cannot stop eating it, even just by the spoonful to 'test' if the balance is correct. Heavenly stuff. Using sourdough adds a nice note. Also, if you happen to have fermented garlic, it works really well in place of regular garlic. SERVES 4 GENEROUSLY

- 200g (7oz) blanched almonds
- 100g (3½oz) stale bread, any really dark crusts removed
- 2–3 garlic cloves, finely grated
- 350–600ml (12–20fl oz) cold water, depending if making sauce or soup
- 2–4 tablespoons sherry vinegar
- 150ml (¼ pint) extra virgin olive oil
- salt and black pepper

To serve, if making sauce
- blanched green veg, such as asparagus, cavolo nero, hispi cabbage, peas, green beans or runner beans
  or
- grilled courgettes, aubergines or blistered tomatoes

To serve, if making soup
- 1 cucumber, peeled and roughly chopped, or ½ sliced diagonally
- drained capers or peas
- torn mint leaves

1. Toast the almonds in a pan for a few minutes until they just start to colour, then tip them on to a plate to cool.

2. Meanwhile, in a blender, combine the almonds, bread and garlic. Blitz until fine crumbs. You will need to scrape down the sides a few times, and it is worth repeating this bit, scraping down the sides and blitzing again, as it will give you a smoother end product. When you have a smooth paste, add about 350ml (12fl oz) of the measured cold water a little at a time. I like to stream it in almost as if making a mayonnaise. You may well need to scrape down the sides a couple more times at this stage.

3. Once you get the consistency of a thick yogurt, add in 2 tablespoons of the vinegar and 100ml (3½fl oz) of the extra virgin olive oil in a similar fashion, with a good pinch of salt. Taste and add more salt or vinegar to your taste. It should be luscious and spoonable, but not too thin.

4. If you want more of a soup, add half the cucumber and stream in about another 250ml (9fl oz) of water until you get a thinner (but not watery) consistency. The remaining cucumber should still be able to sit on the surface of the soup.

5. Serve the sauce either underneath or spooned over the blanched or grilled veg like a pillowy blanket, drizzled with the remaining oil and scattered with a few good cracks of black pepper. For the soup, I like to slice the remaining cucumber diagonally and drop it in with a few capers or peas, torn mint leaves and a drizzle of the remaining oil. This is probably the only time I peel a cucumber, but the delicate nature of the soup deserves it.

TOTAL TIME: **30 MINUTES, PLUS SOAKING**

Pickled shiitake sushi rice bowl

We have variations on these a lot, as the rice is the perfect platform for loads of flavour in the form of pickles or ferments, such as sauerkraut or kimchi. I make the mushrooms just to have because they are really tasty. If you, too, like to plan ahead, do the same so that you can whip this dish up even quicker. If using dried shiitake, you can keep their soaking water and use it in place of the measured water.

If there is any leftover rice, the next morning I fry it until crispy, then eat with a fried egg and lots of said pickles and ferments. SERVES 4

1. If your mushrooms are fresh, keep them whole. Put either type of shiitake in a heatproof bowl with the garlic, ginger and bay. In a saucepan, heat the vinegar and measured water. Once at a simmer, dissolve the salt and honey or sugar in it and then pour over the mushrooms. Set aside while you cook the rice.

2. Wash the sushi rice in a bowl of cold water. Give it a shimmy with your fingers to help release more starch. Pour away the starchy water and repeat 3 more times until the water is clear. Tip it into a saucepan with the measured cold water. Leave to soak for 30 minutes. Then cover the pan and bring to a simmer for 10–12 minutes until the water is absorbed; I find 10 minutes is easily enough, but just keep an eye on it. Remove the pan from the heat. Lift the lid and place a folded tea towel over the opening. Replace the lid and leave for 10 minutes.

3. Meanwhile, mix the cabbage, carrot, mayonnaise and sesame seeds together to make a slaw. If you used dried shiitake, now is the time to slice them.

4. Put the rice in bowls with the slaw and mushrooms in piles on top. Sprinkle with togarashi, add the sliced chillies and onions and serve.

For the pickled shiitake
- 100g (3½oz) dried shiitake mushrooms, rehydrated in hot water for 15–30 minutes, or 300g (10½oz) fresh
- 3 garlic cloves, sliced
- 5mm- (¼ inch-) thick slice of fresh root ginger, sliced
- 1 bay leaf
- 125ml (4fl oz) rice vinegar (or white wine vinegar works fine, too)
- 200ml (7fl oz) water
- 1 tablespoon salt
- 1 tablespoon honey, or sugar

For the rice bowl
- 400g (14oz) sushi rice
- 650ml (1 pint 3fl oz) cold water
- 200g (7oz) red cabbage, finely shredded
- 1 large carrot, coarsely grated or finely sliced
- 100g (3½oz) mayonnaise
- 2–3 tablespoons toasted sesame seeds (white and black are good)

To serve
- togarashi seasoning
- sliced red chillies
- finely sliced spring onions, or pickled onions

TOTAL TIME: **10 MINUTES**

Butter beans with torn green olives, almonds & chilli

For impromptu guests, or just as a general midweek life-saver, this is near-endlessly versatile. Serve over a bed of lemon couscous for a more complete meal, or as a side dish, as a starter to keep hungry appetites at bay or piled on to thick-cut toast. All ways, it's a winner.

I love this, too, for side-hustling as a storecupboard dip, if you blend the butter beans instead of serving them whole. Use some of the bean liquid from the can; all of it will be too much, so just add judiciously until it all starts moving in the blender. SERVES 4 AS A SIDE

- 2 × 400g (14oz) cans of butter beans, or 1 large (700g/1lb 9oz) jar, drained
- 100g (3½oz) green olives (I favour Nocellara here for their colour)
- 4–5 tablespoons extra virgin olive oil
- 75g (2¾oz) almonds, roughly chopped
- 1 teaspoon cumin seeds
- 1 generous teaspoon chilli flakes
- 10g (¼oz) mint, leaves picked
- sherry vinegar, or other vinegar, to taste
- sea salt flakes

1. Spread the butter beans out on a serving plate. Remove the stones from the olives and tear the olives randomly. Add on top of the beans.

2. Heat the oil in a small pan, tip in the almonds and toast until golden; 2–3 minutes. When done, turn off the heat and add the cumin seeds and chilli flakes, turning them around in the pan to cook in the residual heat. Spoon the almond mixture over the olives and butter beans and add a sprinkle of sea salt flakes and the mint leaves. Serve with the vinegar sprinkled over, to taste.

MIX & MAKE

TOTAL TIME: **50 MINUTES – 1 HOUR**

Stuffed yogurt flatbreads

These are really quick to make, as you can start cooking the first once it's assembled, then make more: an efficient production line that even children can take part in. They are essentially *lobiani*, by way of Georgia, but with a bit more freshness and zing in the filling. Try to get them fairly thin, as thin as you can as long as the dough doesn't tear.

Use them to fold around a cabbage slaw (such as on page 60) if you want a wrap-type affair, but the filling is in the bread already. MAKES 6

- 600g (1lb 5oz) self-raising flour, or plain flour with 1½ tablespoons baking powder, plus more to dust
- 250g (9oz) yogurt, or kefir, plus extra to serve
- 3 tablespoons olive oil
- 200ml (7fl oz) water

For the stuffing
- 200g (7oz) cherry tomatoes, roughly chopped
- 1 small fennel bulb, finely sliced, tender stalks as well
- juice of 1 lemon
- a little olive oil
- 2 × 400g (14oz) cans of red kidney beans, drained
- salt and black pepper

1. For the stuffing, in a bowl, mix the tomatoes, fennel, lemon juice and a little olive oil together with a pinch of salt. Set aside.

2. Put the flour in a large mixing bowl. Mix the yogurt or kefir with the oil and measured water in a jug, then add it to the flour and knead to combine. Leave the dough to rest while you finish the filling.

3. Add the kidney beans to the tomato mixture and then, with a fork or a masher, crush them up a little, just to help everything bind. Check the seasoning and add salt and pepper accordingly.

4. Divide the rested dough into 6 balls and roll the first out on a floured surface to a diameter of about 24cm (9½ inches). Spoon one-sixth of the filling into the middle, pat it down a little, then start folding in the dough to the centre around the filling; 6–8 folds should be sufficient. Now squeeze the edges to seal the filling inside, flip the bread over and gently roll out back to around 20cm (8 inches) in diameter.

5. Cook for about 5 minutes on each side in a dry frying pan over a medium–low heat, while you repeat to form and fill the next flatbread. Repeat until they are all done. You can keep them warm in a low oven, or reheat quickly in the pan. Serve warm with extra yogurt or kefir.

TOTAL TIME: **30 MINUTES**

Speedy falafels

As you might imagine, these started off as a way of quickly getting a sort-of falafel fix. By all means, press them down when cooking, but they work well as they are now also. I use canned chickpeas here, as I want that slightly undercooked texture. To simulate the texture and taste of fresh falafels, I find crushing them with your hands and adding gram flour is a good way to stop them falling apart, as well as not turning into a paste. This is one of those occasions where you can use up all the ends of herbs, if you have them, in the fridge drawer.

MAKES 8 LARGE OR 16 SMALL

- 2 × 400g (14oz) cans of chickpeas, drained
- 1 onion, roughly chopped
- 1 tablespoon ground coriander
- 1 teaspoon ground cumin
- 100g (3½oz) gram (chickpea) flour
- 50g (1¾oz) soft herbs, such as coriander, parsley, mint or dill, roughly chopped
- 1 tablespoon baking powder
- flavourless oil, for frying
- salt
- flatbreads or pittas and diced tomatoes, to serve

For the pickled red onions
- finely grated zest and juice of 2 lemons
- 1 red onion, finely sliced
- 1 tablespoon sumac, plus extra to garnish
- 1 cucumber, shaved into ribbons with a veg peeler

For the tahini sauce
- 75g (2¾oz) tahini
- 1 garlic clove, finely grated

1. To make the pickled red onions, add half the lemon zest and juice to the red onion in a small bowl with the sumac and a pinch of salt. Set aside.

2. Mix the tahini in a small bowl with the remaining lemon juice, the garlic and a good pinch of salt. Loosen the sauce with water a little at a time until a thick cream texture is achieved. (If it gets too thin, you can always add a bit more tahini.)

3. Put the chickpeas in a large mixing bowl with the onion, spices, gram flour, herbs and baking powder, adding a good pinch of salt. Crush with your hands until you get a rough crumb that starts to hold together; texture is good, so don't go too far, but make sure the mixture is crushed enough to hold together when frying.

4. Divide the falafel mixture into 8 large or 16 smaller pucks, packing them together tightly. The flat edge helps them crisp in the pan and also aids in them not falling apart. Heat 2–3 tablespoons of oil in a large frying pan over a medium heat and add the falafels to the pan, but don't overcrowd it. You may have to fry these in 2 batches, especially as you are going to gently but assertively crush each to about 2.5cm (1 inch) thick as you fry on each side until crisp and golden; 3–4 minutes a side. Remove to a plate lined with kitchen paper while you fry the rest, adding a little more oil to the pan.

5. Meanwhile, toss the cucumber together with the pickled onions.

6. Serve the falafels with flatbreads or stuffed inside pittas, accompanied by the pickled onions and cucumber, the tahini sauce and diced tomatoes, sprinkled with extra sumac.

TOTAL TIME: **25–30 MINUTES**

Crispy noodle omelette

This is a bit of a mash-up of different influences and cuisines, born out of leftovers and a need for a tasty dinner. Crispy noodles bound with egg make for a lovely platform to soak up all the flavours you throw at it. You can make it straight through by soaking noodles in boiling water, draining and cooling, but I also like to make extra at dinner, knowing I can have this the next day. If you want a lighter meal, you can get by with making this with just one egg per person.

Have a look for bean sprouts in a jar, as they last a lot longer and are always to hand. SERVES 4

- flavourless oil, for cooking
- 200g (7oz) rice noodles, cooked according to the packet instructions, then drained, cooled under cold water and drained well again
- 8 eggs (or see recipe introduction)
- 4 spring onions, finely sliced
- 15g (½oz) coriander, leaves picked
- 10g (¼oz) mint, leaves picked
- 1–2 red or green chillies, sliced (optional)
- 330g (11½oz) jar of bean sprouts (optional)
- salt
- sriracha, or hot sauce, to serve (for homemade hot sauce, see page 75)

For the sauce
(all ingredients to taste)
- 4 tablespoons soy sauce
- 2–3 tablespoons rice vinegar
- 1 thumb of fresh root ginger, peeled and finely grated
- 2 garlic cloves, finely grated

1. Mix the sauce ingredients together in a bowl, adding more of any ingredient to get the flavour balance you like.

2. I use a 24cm (9½ inch) frying pan for these, as you want enough surface area to get a nice crunch going on the noodles. Heat 2–3 tablespoons of oil in the pan over a medium–high heat. Add the noodles and spread them out. Leave them to cook and crisp slightly for 3–4 minutes, but watch that they don't catch. Give them a toss or a flip to continue cooking the soft side; another 3–4 minutes should be good. Remove to a plate.

3. In a mixing bowl, beat 2 eggs, add one-quarter of the spring onion and a good pinch of salt, followed by one-quarter of the crisped-up noodles.

4. Heat 1 tablespoon of oil in the frying pan over a medium heat. Add the omelette mix and spread it out evenly in the pan. Cook for 2–3 minutes until set on the first side, then flip over. Reduce the heat if you feel it is cooking too fast. Cook until the egg is set through, then remove to a plate. Keep this warm in a low oven while you repeat the process to make 3 more omelettes.

5. Add one-quarter of the herbs, chilli and bean sprouts, if using, to each omelette then fold over. Serve with the sauce, with sriracha or hot sauce on the side, if you like.

MIX & MAKE

TOTAL TIME: **45 MINUTES**

Monster pea & potato croquettes

What beats croquettes? One massive one all to yourself, that's what. As you are cooking large croquettes here, using more oil isn't such a big deal because of the reduction in surface area, so just drain them well on kitchen paper and get stuck in.

You can fry these without so much oil, too – you just have to watch them for catching and burning, almost toasting them in the pan until golden. Then cook them through in an oven preheated to 200°C/180°C fan (400°F), Gas Mark 6 for 15–20 minutes. SERVES 4

- 250g (9oz) frozen peas, preferably petits pois
- 800g (1lb 12oz) cold mashed potato, made from fluffy starchy potatoes (not waxy ones)
- 150g (5½oz) Cheddar cheese, coarsely grated, or cut into small cubes
- 2–3 eggs
- 50g (1¾oz) flour
- 200g (7oz) breadcrumbs
- flavourless oil, for frying
- salt and black pepper

For the salad
- 1 banana shallot, finely sliced
- 15g (½oz) parsley, leaves picked
- 15g (½oz) mint, leaves picked
- handful of finely chopped chives (optional)
- 2 tablespoons olive oil
- 1 tablespoon vinegar (red or white wine or cider vinegar are all fine)

1. Boil a kettle. Defrost the peas by tipping them into a large heatproof mixing bowl and pouring over boiling water. After 5 minutes, drain well. Mix with the mashed potato and Cheddar, and season with salt and a few good grinds of black pepper. Divide into 4 and shape each into a puck about 15 × 10cm (6 × 4 inches).

2. Lightly beat 2 of the eggs and put on a small baking tray or plate. (Beat in the last later on if you need it.) Put the flour and breadcrumbs on 2 separate plates.

3. Carefully drop each croquette into the flour and turn over once or twice, patting to coat entirely in flour. Brush off any excess. Next, add them to the egg to coat fully. Then coat carefully in the breadcrumbs. Pat them all over: all the surface needs to be covered with crumbs without any holes.

4. Heat about 2.5cm (1 inch) of oil in a heavy-based saucepan. Carefully lower in 2 croquettes and fry for 3–4 minutes on each side until golden and crisp. Remove to a plate lined with kitchen paper. They can be kept warm in a low oven while you cook the rest.

5. Meanwhile, for the salad, mix the shallot, herbs, olive oil and vinegar with a pinch of salt. Serve the croquettes with the salad piled on top.

TOTAL TIME: TORTILLAS: 30–50 MINUTES, PLUS RESTING; QUESADILLAS: 6–10 MINUTES EXTRA PER QUESADILLA

Homemade tortillas (for quesadillas)

I often turn to these tortillas if I don't have any bread but still want a sandwich. Feel free to use just plain flour, but I like adding a little rye or wholemeal for extra flavour. These make particularly good quesadillas.

If you have tortillas left over – either these or any other wraps – brush them lightly with oil, cut into triangles or strips, lay on a baking tray and toast in an oven preheated to 200°C/180°C fan (400°F), Gas Mark 6 for 12–15 minutes until golden and crisp (check them after 8 minutes). Use them for dipping, or as a crunchy topping on soups or stews.

As an alternative filling, I like to use the bean salad on page 12, assembling it while the dough is resting, to have a more substantial meal ready in no time. MAKES 10 TORTILLAS

For the tortillas
- 400g (14oz) plain flour, plus more to dust
- 200g (7oz) wholemeal flour, or rye flour
- 4 tablespoons oil (olive or sunflower works well)
- 150ml (¼ pint) lukewarm water
- good pinch of salt

For the quesadillas (optional), enough to fill all 10 tortillas to make 5 quesadillas
- 250g (9oz) Cheddar cheese, grated
- 2 peppers (any colour), cored, deseeded and chopped
- 1 red onion, chopped
- 1–2 green or red chillies, finely chopped
- hot sauce, to serve (for homemade, see page 75)

1. Either in a stand mixer fitted with the dough hook or a mixing bowl, combine all the ingredients for the tortillas. Mix well to form a dough. If using a mixer, knead the dough for 5 minutes until smooth and coming away from the sides of the bowl. If hand kneading, turn it out on to a work surface and knead for 5–8 minutes until smooth. Either way, place on a work surface with the upturned bowl over it and leave to rest for 15 minutes.

2. Warm a large frying pan over a medium–low heat.

3. Divide the dough, either by eye or by weighing each piece, into 10 equal pieces. Dust a work surface lightly with flour and roll out each ball evenly. Go as thin as you can without breaking the dough; 20–24cm (8–9½ inches) should be about right. Lift the tortilla carefully into the pan to cook.

4. Cook each tortilla for 1–2 minutes on each side until starting to bubble and brown slightly. Keep the cooked tortillas wrapped in a clean tea towel while you cook the rest. You can roll the next as the first is in the pan, and so on.

5. If making the quesadillas, mix the cheese, peppers, onion and chilli together. Divide between 5 tortillas equally. Place the remaining 5 tortillas on top of the cheese mixture. Heat the same pan used to make the tortillas over a low heat (enlist a second pan to speed things up and cook 2 at once, if you like). Add a quesadilla and cook each side for 3–5 minutes until the cheese has melted and the tortilla is crisp. Cut up and serve while you cook the rest.

MIX & MAKE

TOTAL TIME: **40 MINUTES**

Canned fruit hot sauce (canned heat)

This is a great recipe to make ahead, to ensure you have a big punch of flavour to bring dishes alive. Using canned fruit means that those tropical flavours are always at hand. Have a play with which fruit you use; I like this blend between mango and pineapple, as it adds a little complexity. As you may notice, this hot sauce finds itself on many plates in this book. If you use fresh chillies, the heat will be more prominent. I use the larger amount of chillies here, but if you want it to be fruitier, reduce the amount; you'll still have the chilli kick but more fruitiness.

Equally, make your own pickled chillies. Heat a 50:50 water-to-vinegar ratio in a saucepan with a good teaspoon or so of salt, then pour over a packed sterilized jar of chillies to cover. Seal and leave in the fridge for a week to pickle. Or leave them longer out of the fridge and they will start to ferment. If you have the patience and use these fermented chillies, the sauce is taken to another level. MAKES ABOUT 1.5KG (3LB 5OZ) SAUCE

- 2 tablespoons olive oil
- 2 onions, roughly chopped
- 4 garlic cloves, peeled
- 2 × 400g (14oz) cans of plum tomatoes
- 400g (14oz) can of mango
- 400g (14oz) can of pineapple
- 100–200g (3½–7oz) pickled or fermented red chillies, or fresh red chillies (see recipe introduction), stalks removed, roughly chopped
- 2–3½ tablespoons wine vinegar, or cider vinegar, to taste
- salt

1. Heat the oil in a large saucepan over a medium heat and add the onions. Reduce the heat to medium–low and cook for 10–15 minutes until the onions are translucent. I put a lid on the pan to help the onions become sweet. You want them cooked through and soft, without much colour.

2. Add the rest of the ingredients except the vinegar and salt to the pan, breaking up the tomatoes roughly with a wooden spoon. Bring to a simmer and bubble away for 20 minutes. Give it a stir every now and again.

3. Meanwhile, run the jars or bottles you intend to store the sauce in through the hot cycle of the dishwasher and allow them to steam-dry in there until you're ready for them.

4. Scrape the mixture from the pan into a blender with a good 2 pinches of salt, going carefully as it is hot, then blend until smooth. Taste and add vinegar and salt to your taste. Blend again. Taste again. Adjust further: it wants to be right on the edge of too much salt and vinegar, as when it chills and settles they will integrate into the sauce. Pour the sauce into the sterilized jars or bottles, then seal and allow to cool to room temperature for a couple of hours. Store in the fridge for easily 3 months or so.

5. I then decant the sauce currently open into a saved and washed squeezy bottle for easy use.

on SEASONING

This chapter is full of meals that are brought to life by seasonings: pickled shiitakes enlivening sushi rice bowls, two coconut chutneys bringing pea pancakes with potato curry to life or a herby shallot salad piled over super-sized croquettes.

'Seasoning' can refer to many things. It can be as simple as salt and pepper, of course, but it's much more than that. Seasoning is that little extra touch that brings a dish, or a whole meal, together.

I must say, I do love a condiment, itself arguably a form of finishing a dish and worthy of consideration in this category. Equally, I usually add a small glass of white wine or cider to any sauce-based dish I'm making; I like that treble note that it brings, providing a sort of bridge to link the other flavours in the recipe together.

However you define 'seasoning', tasting the food you are cooking as you are making it is key. The idea is to layer flavours and seasonings as you go, adding specific elements at certain times to get the desired effect you are after.

Whenever you are unsure how to season a dish, take a spoonful out and put it on a plate. Consider it. Now add what you think it needs: perhaps salt, acid in the form of vinegar or lemon juice or even a herb. Taste, then if it is to your liking, proceed to season the whole dish accordingly, or try again with something else if not. Sometimes you may also find it is good as it is and you may be overcomplicating things. Recognizing when to stop is an equally important skill.

For me, most dishes will be anointed with a glug of extra virgin olive oil; they also receive a crowning splash of vinegar. The oil adds a richness and helps everything marry on the plate, while the vinegar brings the excitement and pep. Sometimes it is just half a capful stirred in at the end of a sauce, soup or stew, but at other times a hearty slosh is needed. I like acid, as does my son, so we tend to be pretty heavy-handed on the vinegar side, often leaving the bottle on the table to be added while eating.

Generally, a few drops of lemon juice improve most things, and I like to serve lemon wedges alongside many dishes. It is a gentler acid than vinegar and equally helps lift flavours but without taking over.

In France, I found a sea salt blended with dried herbs and vegetables, essentially a stock-flavoured sea salt. The one I use is Herbamare by A Vogel, which is available online, but there are others. I use it for omelettes, simply sprinkled on tomatoes or in rice, where the stock flavour really comes through. Basically, anywhere you would use salt it adds a little extra and is a trusty go-to for a flavour boost. You could make your own by drying out veg peelings and/or herbs in a low oven, blending to a fine powder, then stirring into salt.

In terms of regular salt, if you are worried about adding too much to a dish, hold off and season at the last minute instead. That way, the salt flavour is more prominent, as it hasn't been absorbed by the food and muted. I did this when weaning my son, so he had little salt, and I would then add a bit more to my food. I found that overall I was having a lot less salt. You may find you need to add a pinch more salt to leftovers, to wake them up again.

I like to keep the milder Korean chilli flakes to hand, to add a little warmth to a dish without blowing it out of proportion pepper-spice-wise. The little red flakes also add a pleasing colour.

But the main pillar of 'seasoning', whatever that may be, is to taste. Always taste as you go. Adjust the seasoning according to what you think a dish needs while keeping the finished, potentially reduced (thus flavour-concentrated) dish in mind. Experiment. Try new things. Find out what you like and lean into it, then build your seasoning around what is most favoured by you and those you eat with.

ONE POT ON THE HOB

My favourite way to cook, there is something so grounding about a pot of nourishing food in the middle of the table. These are dishes that are designed to satisfy everyone, generously proportioned as well as packed out with fragrant flavour, with variations to suit seasonal ingredients and settings. I've also included a couple of speedy save-the-day options for good measure. And minimal washing-up anyone?!

TOTAL TIME: **30 MINUTES**

Coconut & lime leaf broth with rice noodles

Serve this dish with something tangy and/or fresh to cut the richness. I've suggested thinly sliced green tomatoes, but as they aren't available most of the year, use what is. Thinly sliced gooseberries would be brilliant, for instance, or something pickled, such as thin slices of radish, which have the added advantage of being available year-round.

For the quick-pickled cucumbers, bring 150ml (¼ pint) each of vinegar and water to the boil in a saucepan. Add 1 crushed garlic clove, 1 bay leaf, 1 teaspoon of sugar or honey and a healthy pinch of salt. Drop in 1 cucumber, cut whichever way you prefer (I like simple slices), turn off the heat and set aside until you are ready to serve. This keeps well for a week or so in the fridge. SERVES 4

1. Set a large saucepan over a medium heat and add 2–3 tablespoons of oil. Follow with the lemongrass, garlic, ginger and lime leaves. Cook, stirring, for 1–2 minutes until aromatic. Add the turmeric and the coconut milk along with the courgette, onion, carrots and canned tomatoes. Bring to a bubble and cook until the courgette is tender; 6–8 minutes should be good.

2. Season with lime juice to taste, check the salt and adjust if needed.

3. Divide the noodles between warmed bowls and top with the soup. I like the noodles cold here, as they cool down the soup, but if you want them warming you can refresh them in boiling water and drain well again. Serve with the chillies, tomatoes or pickled cucumber slices, herbs and lime wedges for squeezing over.

- 2–3 tablespoons flavourless oil (I use sunflower oil)
- 3 lemongrass stalks, bashed to help them release flavour
- 3 garlic cloves, finely grated or crushed
- 1 thumb of fresh root ginger, peeled and finely grated
- 5 lime leaves
- 1 heaped teaspoon ground turmeric
- 2 × 400g (14oz) cans of coconut milk
- 200g (7oz) courgette, cut into 1cm (½ inch) pieces
- 1 onion, sliced
- 2 carrots, sliced
- 400g (14oz) can of plum tomatoes, crushed up
- juice of 2–3 limes, to taste, plus lime wedges to serve
- 300g (10½oz) rice noodles, cooked according to the packet instructions, then drained, cooled under cold water and drained well again
- salt

To serve
- 2 red chillies, finely sliced
- handful of green tomatoes, finely sliced (or see recipe introduction), or quick-pickled cucumbers, sliced (see recipe introduction)
- handful of soft herbs, such as dill, coriander or basil

TOTAL TIME: 45–50 MINUTES, PLUS SOAKING, FOR DRIED BEANS; 15 MINUTES FOR CANNED BEANS

Hannah's rosemary pinto beans

This is my friend Hannah Fuellenkemper's 'no-recipe bean recipe'. It isn't really a recipe as such, more a preparation for beans that is simple and tasty. I will have leftover cooked beans in the fridge ready to go on most days, as I always double- or triple-batch cook them. They heat up in a moment and go with most things. The cooking method can be applied to other dried beans, and Hannah's favourite are borlotti (see pages 166–7). I ate these with Hannah the first time we met, when we both provided elements for a lunch, with everything getting piled into a bowl. Once you have your solid foundation of simply well-cooked beans, the world is open for whichever wonderful way you want to top them. On that first meeting, we had soft-boiled eggs, poached baby leeks and pickled red onions, to name a few bits. Poached veg, used as is or griddled or fried for extra colour and flavour, is great. SERVES 8

1. Set a large saucepan over a medium heat and add the oil. Add the garlic and rosemary and cook for 1 minute, then follow with the soaked and drained beans and measured water. Bring to a simmer.

2. Cook until tender. This could take 30–40 minutes if the beans are relatively fresh, or it may take a touch longer if they are older.

3. If using canned beans, add them with their juice from the cans and gently bubble for just 5 minutes.

4. Pour in the wine and add a good pinch of salt, then return to a simmer for 5 minutes. Serve with whatever toppings you like, finished with a good grind of black pepper, or cool and keep for another meal.

- 2–4 tablespoons olive oil
- 5 garlic cloves, sliced
- 1 large rosemary sprig
- 500g (1lb 2oz) dried pinto beans, soaked overnight or for 8 hours (see pages 166–7), drained, or 4 × 400g (14oz) cans
- 1.5 litres (2¾ pints) water, if using soaked dried beans
- 200ml (7fl oz) white wine
- salt and black pepper

To serve (all just suggestions)
- boiled eggs
- grilled baby leeks
- blanched veg, such as green beans
- pickled red cabbage and/or onions (for homemade, see pages 110 and 89)

ONE POT ON THE HOB

TOTAL TIME: 45–55 MINUTES

Spelt stew au pistou

A chuck-it-in-the-pot-while-you-chop-some-veg type of thing, really nourishing and warming, with the pistou as a lovely foil. The pistou recipe here will most likely give you more than you require for this meal, but you need a certain volume of ingredients to get everything turning in the blender or food processor (or indeed amalgamating in the mortar, if you're feeling energetic). Store any leftovers in a container in the fridge with a little extra oil poured over the top to stop it oxidizing. You can use it on everything and anything: on fried eggs in the morning; tossed with beans and veg as a dressing... anywhere you'd use extra virgin olive oil. I set the blender jug on a set of scales and measure the oil directly into it, for ease. SERVES 4–6 GENEROUSLY

- 2 tablespoons flavourless oil, such as sunflower
- 1 onion, finely chopped
- 1 carrot, finely chopped (optional)
- 1 small fennel bulb, finely chopped
- 3 garlic cloves, sliced
- 150g (5½oz) pearled spelt
- 1 litre (1¾ pints) water
- 2 courgettes, chopped into 1cm (½ inch) pieces
- 2 × 400g (14oz) cans of white beans, or 250g (9oz) dried beans, soaked overnight or for 8 hours, cooked and drained (see pages 166–7)
- 200g (7oz) fine green beans, finely chopped
- 1 tablespoon white or red wine vinegar, or cider vinegar
- salt and black pepper
- grated hard cheese, to serve

For the pistou
- 50g (1¾oz) basil
- 3 garlic cloves
- 100ml (3½fl oz) extra virgin olive oil

1. Set a large saucepan that will fit everything over a medium–low heat and warm up the flavourless oil. Add the onion, carrot, if using, and fennel with a good pinch of salt. Cook for 10–12 minutes until soft and translucent, adding the garlic for the last couple of minutes.

2. Meanwhile, make your pistou. Feel free to use a pestle and mortar, though I use a blender or small food processor for speed. Put the basil, garlic and oil in a blender with a pinch of salt and blitz to a sauce.

3. Add the spelt and measured water to the large saucepan and cook for 25–35 minutes or until tender. Once the spelt is cooked, add the courgettes and cook for 2 minutes. Follow with the white beans, adding the liquid from the cans if using canned (if using dried beans, just add an extra 300ml/½ pint of water), and green beans, and cook for a further minute or so until the green beans are just tender. Add the vinegar, check the seasoning and add salt and black pepper accordingly.

4. Serve the stew with the pistou to dollop on top – or stir it through the stew if you prefer.

ONE POT ON THE HOB

TOTAL TIME: 35–40 MINUTES FOR CANNED BEANS;
1 HOUR 5 MINUTES – 1 HOUR 20 MINUTES, PLUS SOAKING, FOR DRIED BEANS

Squash minestrone

I couldn't begin to start counting how many times I've made and eaten this dish; to say it's a go-to is an understatement. I could happily eat it every day. We used to eat a similar version as a family when I was a child, which I have carried on making. I know it sounds odd to some people, but the leftovers from dinner make the best breakfast. For me, it's the perfect way to start the day, or to end it, for that matter. If made ahead, minestrone just gets better the longer it sits. Dare I say double-batch?

I took the minestrone in the photo camping with us. A quick reheat and we had a nourishing and warming meal in the drizzly Suffolk countryside.

SERVES 4 GENEROUSLY

1. Set a large saucepan that will fit everything over a medium heat with the olive oil. Add the onion, celery and carrots with a good pinch of salt and cook for 8–10 minutes until beginning to soften. Add the bay, rosemary, garlic and leek and cook for a further 3 minutes.

2. Now add the tomatoes and crush them up a little with a wooden spoon. Follow with the squash or pumpkin, pour in the measured water and bring to a simmer. Cook for 7–10 minutes. Then add the beans, adding the liquid from the cans if using canned (if using dried beans, just add an extra 300–400ml/10–14fl oz of water), and the pasta. Return to a simmer and cook until the pasta is al dente, according to the packet instructions, though it will keep cooking after you take it off the heat, so err on the only-just-cooked side.

3. Stir in the parsley, then check and adjust the seasoning with salt and pepper. Serve with grated cheese, extra virgin olive oil, lemon wedges to squeeze over and crusty bread.

- 2 tablespoons olive oil
- 1 onion, roughly chopped
- 2 celery sticks, sliced
- 2 small carrots, chopped
- 1 bay leaf
- 1 rosemary sprig
- 3 garlic cloves, sliced
- 1 leek, cleaned and roughly sliced
- 400g (14oz) can of plum tomatoes
- 500g (1lb 2oz) prepared squash or pumpkin, cut into cubes
- 1.5 litres (2¾ pints) water
- 2 × 400g (14oz) cans of beans (borlotti, red kidney, cannellini or a mix), or 250g (9oz) dried beans, soaked overnight or for 8 hours, cooked and drained (see pages 166–7)
- 100g (3½oz) pasta (ideally small shapes, such as shells)
- 15g (½oz) parsley, leaves picked and finely chopped
- salt and black pepper

To serve
- grated hard cheese, such as Spenwood
- extra virgin olive oil
- lemon wedges
- crusty bread

TOTAL TIME: **10–15 MINUTES**

Cheesy French toast with sweetcorn salsa

This is one of those dishes that you daydream about eating again while you are still enjoying it. It's really comforting while being good for you, too.

Have a play with the pickles and ferments you add to the salsa, to fit your tastes, or if you don't have pickled onions or gherkins, just thinly slice half a small red onion and put it in a bowl with 1–2 tablespoons of red wine vinegar and a good pinch of salt. Set aside for 10–15 minutes, then continue to make the salsa. SERVES 1

- 2 small eggs
- 2 tablespoons milk
- 50g (1¾oz) hard cheese, such as Cheddar, grated
- 1 thick slice of bread, preferably sourdough
- 1 tablespoon oil, or butter
- salt
- hot sauce, to serve (for homemade, see page 75)

For the sweetcorn salsa
- 100g (3½oz) frozen sweetcorn kernels, or canned (drained weight)
- 1 tablespoon roughly chopped parsley leaves (or other herbs work fine)
- 2 tablespoons pickled onions, or chopped gherkins (or see recipe introduction)

1. In a wide dish, beat the eggs with the milk, the cheese and a good pinch of salt. Add the slice of bread and turn to cover evenly. Leave to soak up as much of the egg mixture as possible.

2. Meanwhile, make the sweetcorn salsa. If using frozen sweetcorn, pour hot water over the kernels in a heatproof bowl until well submerged. Leave to defrost for 5 minutes, then drain. Whichever sweetcorn you are using, mix it with the parsley and pickled onions.

3. Set a frying pan over a medium–low heat, add the oil or butter, then follow with the soaked slice of bread. I spoon a little the remaining egg mixture over the slice as it cooks until it is all in the pan. Do this evenly. No rush. Cook gently for about 2–3 minutes on each side until golden and set.

4. Serve with the sweetcorn salsa and a spicy condiment of your liking.

ONE POT ON THE HOB

TOTAL TIME: 35–40 MINUTES

Garlic-chilli potato dumplings

These make a pretty quick and comforting dinner. My kids really like them and they are super versatile. It doesn't really matter what shape they end up – fat, thin, short or long dumplings – they taste just as good and make a fun plate.

This one-pot recipe is designed for using up ready-cooked potatoes. However, if you don't have any in the fridge, you can boil the same quantity, peeled and quartered, for 12–15 minutes until tender, then chill them under a cold tap.

If I am in a rush I like to roll out the dough with a rolling pin then make criss-cross cuts to form little diamonds. Otherwise use good-quality pre-made noodles like udon.

The sauce can be as spicy or not, as you please, and a plateful of steamed green veg goes very well alongside. SERVES 4

For the sauce/dressing
- 30g (1oz) dried shiitake mushrooms
- 200ml (7fl oz) boiling water
- 25g (1oz) coriander, leaves picked, stalks finely chopped, kept separate
- 2 tablespoons tamari sauce
- 5 garlic cloves, finely chopped
- 1 heaped teaspoon chilli flakes
- 100ml (3½oz) sunflower oil
- 25g (1oz) roasted peanuts, chopped
- 3 spring onions, finely sliced

For the dumplings
- 900g (2lb) cooked potatoes, peeled and quartered
- 360g (12¾oz) cornflour, plus more to dust
- salt

1. For the sauce/dressing, put the shiitake in a small heatproof bowl and pour in the measured boiling water from the kettle. Leave to rehydrate while you make and cook the dumplings.

2. To make the dumplings, push the cooked potatoes through a ricer, or use a masher to crush them. Add the cornflour with a pinch of salt and form into a smooth dough. Pinch off the dough in sections and roll each out on a lightly floured surface to form ropes.

3. Cut along the lengths to form 1cm (½ inch) dumplings; I like a 5cm- (2 inch-) long, fat dumpling. Place on a lightly floured tray and repeat the process until the dough is all shaped.

4. Bring a large saucepan of well-salted water to a simmer. Add your dumplings, wait for them to float to the surface, then cook for 1–2 minutes. Drain well and put in a heatproof mixing bowl.

5. Drain and slice the rehydrated shiitake, then add to the mixing bowl with the coriander stalks and tamari. Finally, add the garlic and chilli flakes in a small pile.

6. Heat the oil in a small pan. Pour the hot oil over the garlic and chilli to let both sizzle and cook. Toss, then serve topped with the peanuts, spring onions and coriander leaves.

TOTAL TIME: 35–45 MINUTES, PLUS COOLING

Tuscan spelt salad: summer version

This is one of those dishes that signifies summer for me. It used to be on the menu when I worked at Towpath Café, and whenever it was, it was always my lunch. It has lots of pops of fresh flavours with a good hearty base of spelt, which together keep you refreshed but full in the warmer months.

I also made this when I was on my honeymoon in the USA; we took it out on a hike, as it is easy to transport and a perfect out-and-about lunch, or even camping dinner, that just gets better once it sits for a while. If I haven't sold it to you yet, just make it: you will enjoy it! SERVES 4

- 270g (9½oz) pearled spelt
- 200g (7oz) frozen peas, preferably petits pois
- 1 cucumber, cut into 1cm (½ inch) pieces, excessive seeds removed
- 400g (14oz) cherry tomatoes, halved across their equator
- 200g (7oz) radishes, sliced
- 25g (1oz) basil, leaves picked, large ones roughly torn
- juice of 2 lemons, or to taste
- 2 tablespoons extra virgin olive oil, or to taste
- chilli flakes (optional)
- **salt and black pepper**

1. Cook the spelt in a pan of well-salted water until tender; 30–40 minutes should do. Drain well and spread out on a tray to cool.

2. Meanwhile, put the peas in a large heatproof bowl. Pour a kettle of boiling water over them and leave to sit for a few minutes until defrosted. Drain and refresh under cold running water, then drain well again and transfer to a mixing bowl.

3. Combine the cooled spelt, salad vegetables and basil with the drained peas. Add half the lemon juice, a good pinch of salt and a few twists of black pepper with the extra virgin olive oil. Taste and add more seasoning, lemon juice and oil if it needs it, as well as chilli flakes, if you want. I tend to hold back on the oil and dress plates individually, as spelt has the tendency to soak up masses of oil.

TOTAL TIME: **40-50 MINUTES**

Tuscan spelt salad: Autumn version

This version enables you to enjoy spelt salad all year round. Serving it warmer makes it a welcome comfort dish in the colder months. However, allow to cool a little and serve at room temperature if you are lucky enough to have a bit of an Indian summer. Add caramelized onions or dried fruits for another dimension, or favourite spices would be lovely here. Try roasting the squash with cumin and fennel seeds for the last few minutes of cooking.

This recipe is breaking the 'rules' of the chapter by its presence, as it involves a tray in the oven. But it seemed useful to have it next to its summer cousin, so here it is! SERVES 4

- 270g (9½oz) pearled spelt
- 200g (7oz) cavolo nero, or kale, leaves only, roughly chopped
- 2 red onions, each cut into 8
- 400g (14oz) prepared squash or pumpkin, cut into 1cm (½ inch) cubes
- 2–3 tablespoons olive oil
- 200g (7oz) cooked chestnuts, crumbled
- 25g (1oz) parsley, finely chopped
- 3 tablespoons red wine vinegar, or to taste
- 5 tablespoons extra virgin olive oil, or to taste
- chilli flakes (optional)
- salt and black pepper

1. Preheat the oven to 220°C/200°C fan (425°F), Gas Mark 7.

2. Cook the spelt in a pan of well-salted boiling water until tender; 30–40 minutes should do. Add the cavolo nero or kale for the last minute of cooking. Drain well and, if you prefer a cooler salad, spread out on a tray to cool.

3. While the spelt is cooking, toss the onions and squash or pumpkin in the olive oil. Spread out on a baking tray and roast in the oven until golden and soft – 25–35 minutes – flipping the veg around after 15 minutes to help it cook evenly.

4. Mix the spelt and cavolo nero or kale with the roast veg and add the chestnuts and parsley. Season with the vinegar and extra virgin olive oil to taste, along with salt and black pepper, adding chilli flakes if you want, then serve.

TOTAL TIME: **50 MINUTES – 1 HOUR**

Peas-otto

Here is a fun way to serve split peas, providing a lovely base that lends itself to smooth veg sauces, or lots of toppings (if you're willing to break free of the one-pot rule of this chapter, that is!), just like a risotto would but with less fat or richness. You can throw your favourite things at this, whether they be vinegar-spiked, crunchy, roasted or raw. If using yellow split peas, the pea-sotto works particularly well with purées of broccoli or roasted squash stirred in at the end. It is also a great dish to have ready in the fridge, as it reheats in moments.
I must admit I do like it spread – chilled – on hot toast. SERVES 4

- 2–3 tablespoons olive oil, or other good oil
- 1 onion, chopped
- 1 leek, cleaned and chopped
- 2 garlic cloves, finely sliced
- 250g (9oz) green or yellow split peas
- 120ml (4fl oz) white wine, or cider
- 1.2 litres (2 pints) hot vegetable stock
- 40g (1½oz) unsalted butter (optional)
- 100g (3½oz) or so of hard cheese, such as Spenwood, finely grated
- salt and black pepper

To add (these are only suggestions; see recipe introduction)
- vegetable purées
- roast squash
- roast broccoli
- blanched asparagus

1. Take a large saucepan that will fit everything and place over a medium–low heat with the oil. Add the onion and cook for 8–10 minutes. Once softened, add the leek and garlic and cook for a further 5 minutes. Stir in the split peas, then pour in the wine or cider and bring to a simmer over a medium heat.

2. Pour in the hot stock, bring to a simmer and cook for 30–40 minutes until the split peas are tender.

3. Stir in the butter, if using, and the cheese. Taste for seasoning and add salt and pepper to taste (it will probably take quite a bit of seasoning). At this point, if using a veg purée or chunks of roast or blanched veg, stir them through and serve.

ONE POT ON THE HOB

TOTAL TIME: 35–40 MINUTES

Broccoli & spelt hotcakes

Between the grated courgette and the spelt flour, these end up with a lovely custardy texture, and, spiked with loads of greens, they are really satisfying at any time of day. I often make them for breakfast for the family, as they come together so easily and don't take long to cook. As well as breakfast, they work well in packed lunches or as dinner, perhaps with a bean salad alongside (see pages 12 and 18) and/or your favourite sauce.

If you don't have any leftover broccoli or other pre-cooked veg in the fridge, simply blanch it in a saucepan of well-salted boiling water for about 4–5 minutes until tender, then refresh under cold running water. A sweet potato, coarsely grated and stirred into the beaten eggs, also works really well.

Cheese is a nice addition to this, too, so mix in 200g (7oz) of cubed feta, if you have some and feel like it. MAKES 8

- 1 head of broccoli (450–500g/ 1lb–1lb 2oz), blanched and chilled
- 2 courgettes, total weight about 300g (10½oz), coarsely grated
- 200g (7oz) frozen peas, preferably petits pois, defrosted
- 3 spring onions, finely sliced
- 3 eggs, lightly beaten
- 300g (10½oz) white spelt flour, or other flour
- 1 teaspoon baking powder
- flavourless oil, for frying
- salt

1. Roughly chop the broccoli (slices around 1cm/ ½ inch thick are good) and put it in a mixing bowl with the rest of the veg and the beaten eggs. Follow with the flour and baking powder, as well as a good pinch of salt. Stir gently to combine everything well, then form into 8 pucks.

2. Heat a heavy-based frying pan or flat griddle over a medium–low heat. Add 1–2 tablespoons of oil. If using a frying pan, you will need to cook these in a couple of batches. Cook half the hotcakes for 3–4 minutes on each side until golden and set. They tend to puff up in the middle when cooked through and feel fairly firm to the touch. They should end up being about 3cm (1¼ inch) thick.

3. Keep the finished hotcakes warm in a low oven while you cook the second batch, then serve.

TOTAL TIME: 20–25 MINUTES

Black bean & mushroom ma po

I make this on weekends, piled into a roll or muffin (such as my Malthouse Muffins, see page 46), as a kind of spiced mushroom sloppy Joe; it is satisfyingly messy eating. But it also works well over rice or grains of your choice, with a fried egg and crispy chilli oil on top, for dinner, as in the photo. Any which way you decide to eat this, it is really worth making, as it packs a massive whack of flavour. Adding 300g (10½oz) chopped firm tofu with the ginger and garlic makes it a little more like a traditional *ma po tofu*, and is equally satisfying.

If you can't find chilli bean sauce, swap in a good Chinese chilli sauce or even chilli oil, though in the latter eventuality, reduce the amount of sesame oil. SERVES 4

- 400g (14oz) mushrooms (fresh shiitake, oyster and king oyster are best, but go with what you can get)
- 2 teaspoons Sichuan peppercorns
- 2–3 tablespoons flavourless oil
- 1 large onion, chopped
- ½ thumb of fresh root ginger, peeled and finely grated
- 3 garlic cloves, finely grated
- 2 spring onions, finely sliced, white and green parts kept separate
- 300ml (½ pint) hot vegetable or mushroom stock
- 400g (14oz) can of black beans
- 1 tablespoon cornflour (optional)
- 2 tablespoons chilli bean sauce
- 1–2 tablespoons black vinegar (or sherry vinegar works)
- 1–2 tablespoons toasted sesame oil

To serve (optional)
- cooked rice or grains of your choice
- fried egg
- crispy chilli oil
- coriander leaves

1. Chop or tear the mushrooms into strips, depending on which you are using. Put the Sichuan peppercorns in a dry frying pan over a medium heat and toast for a few minutes, then tip into a mortar and crush them with a pestle.

2. Put the flavourless oil in a large frying pan set over a medium heat. When it's hot, add the mushrooms and onion and cook for 6–8 minutes until soft. Add the ginger, garlic and spring onion whites and cook for 1 minute, then pour in the stock and black beans with the liquid from the can.

3. Bring to a simmer for 2–3 minutes. Add the cornflour, if using, and stir to thicken for a minute. Stir in the Sichuan peppercorns and chilli bean sauce, then the vinegar and sesame oil to taste. Check the seasoning and serve, scattered with the spring onion greens, and coriander, if you like. (To replicate the photo, serve on rice or grains, top with a fried egg and crispy chilli oil, and garnish with coriander.)

ONE POT ON THE HOB

TOTAL TIME: **25 MINUTES**

Chinese-style tomatoey tofu scramble

This is loosely based on a Chinese dish of tomato and egg stir-fry, of which I ate a really good version at Silk Road restaurant in South London. There, they serve it over hand-pulled noodles. By all means, do the same. I tend to have this for breakfast, as it's a great start to the day with crusty bread or the previous night's leftover rice, but it's also a most welcome lunch or dinner. SERVES 4 WITH A CARB

- 3–4 tablespoons sunflower oil, or other flavourless oil
- 560g (1lb 4oz) firm tofu
- 2 onions, thickly sliced
- 2 garlic cloves, finely sliced or grated
- 1 thumb of fresh root ginger, peeled and grated or sliced into thin batons
- 1 tablespoon Chinese five spice
- 400g (14oz) can of plum tomatoes
- 3 spring onions, finely sliced
- salt and black pepper
- toasted black or white sesame seeds, to serve

1. Heat 2–3 tablespoons of the oil in a large heavy-based frying pan over a medium/medium–high heat.

2. Drain the tofu. Then, over the pan, crush it in your hands, making sure it is spread out evenly and each piece is in contact with the pan; it doesn't want to be obliterated, but broken down is good. Once it's in the pan, don't touch it. Fry until golden and crisp on the underside; 3–5 minutes.

3. Flip over all the tofu pieces, then add the onions, garlic and ginger. Again, don't move it around; you just want the veg to start to warm and wilt, sitting on top of the tofu. After another 3–5 minutes, when the second side of the tofu pieces is crisp and golden, give everything a stir and cook out the onion a little for a minute or so.

4. Add the five spice and a good pinch of salt, followed by the canned tomatoes, crushing them roughly with a wooden spoon or spatula. Rinse out the tomato can with 100ml (3½fl oz) or so of water, add this to the pan and bring to a simmer, then allow the mixture to reduce for 5 minutes.

5. Stir in most of the spring onions with a few good grinds of black pepper. Check the seasoning and then serve, scattered with the remaining spring onions and the sesame seeds.

ONE POT ON THE HOB

TOTAL TIME: **35 MINUTES**

Sweet potato & sweetcorn fritters

I make these using frozen kernels which, like peas, are a great option. I pour boiling water over the frozen sweetcorn in a heatproof bowl and allow it to sit for 5 minutes before draining. I really like using spelt flour in these fritters, as it gives a texture that is on the cakier side and it means the fritters are more tender. Using wholemeal spelt flour works well, too, though you may need a little more liquid in that case. These go really well with a green tahini sauce. Just blend together 100g (3½oz) tahini with 75–125ml (2½–4fl oz) water, the juice of 1 lemon and 50g (1¾oz) soft herbs, such as coriander and mint.

MAKES 12

- 4 eggs
- 200g (7oz) white spelt flour (or see recipe introduction)
- 2 spring onions, finely sliced
- 25g (1oz) dill, finely chopped
- 350g (12oz) frozen sweetcorn kernels, defrosted, or canned (drained weight)
- 1 sweet potato, about 300g (10½oz), scrubbed and coarsely grated
- 1 teaspoon ground coriander
- 1 teaspoon sweet paprika
- 1 teaspoon baking powder
- flavourless oil, for frying
- salt
- dipping sauce, to serve

1. Lightly beat the eggs in a mixing bowl, then fold in the flour to form a batter. Add the rest of the ingredients except the oil with a good pinch of salt and fold everything together.

2. Set a heavy-based frying pan over a medium–low heat. Add 1 tablespoon of oil, then the batter, using a spoonful for each fritter. Cook as many fritters as can fit comfortably in your pan. I like to flip them once they're set on the underside, after 4–5 minutes, then cook them for a further 3–4 minutes. Don't be shy about flipping them a few times. Once they are golden, slightly puffed in the middle and have a slight resistance when pressed, they are ready. Continue to cook until all 12 fritters are done, adding more oil to the pan with each batch.

3. Serve with a dipping sauce, such as a tahini sauce blitzed up with soft herbs to make it green (see recipe introduction).

TOTAL TIME: **30–35 MINUTES**

Shortcut ratatouille sauce

A speedy ratatouille; cutting the veg into a dice is a little cheffy, but it does speed the cooking up a great deal. Serve simply with a chunk of bread or transform into a makeshift shakshuka by adding spices to the pan and then cracking in some eggs.

I like this piled on to pre-cooked barley for dinner, or with the barley mixed through the veg for a packed lunch. Ratatouille is such a showcase of summer produce; simple, but always the best.

SERVES 4

- 5 tablespoons extra virgin olive oil, plus more (optional) to serve
- 1 large aubergine, cut into a 1cm (½ inch) dice
- 2 peppers (any colour), cored, deseeded and cut into 1cm (½ inch) dice
- 2 onions, roughly chopped
- 2 courgettes, cut into 1cm (½ inch) dice
- 3 garlic cloves, sliced
- 400g (14oz) cherry tomatoes, quartered, or regular tomatoes, chopped
- splash of red wine vinegar, to taste
- 25g (1oz) basil, leaves picked, stalks finely chopped
- sea salt flakes and black pepper

To serve (optional)
- cooked pearled barley, or other grains such as pearled spelt or oat groats
- grated hard cheese, such as Spenwood

1. Heat a wide pan over a medium heat. Add half the oil and then the aubergine. Cook for 2–3 minutes, then add the peppers with a good pinch of salt. Cook for a further 5–7 minutes until soft and cooked through, then tip into a bowl.

2. Add the remaining oil to the pan. Once heated, add the onions with another pinch of salt and cook for 5 minutes, then follow with the courgettes and garlic, cooking for a further 5–7 minutes until soft and with a little colour. Add the tomatoes and cook for a further 5–7 minutes until those are collapsing.

3. Stir the aubergine and peppers through the veg in the pan, adding the vinegar to your taste and the basil stalks. Check for salt and add more if needed along with black pepper. Serve on warm cooked grains, with grated cheese and extra virgin olive oil, if you like, scattered with the basil leaves.

TOTAL TIME: **15 MINUTES**

Onion cheese on toast

Before anyone asks why we need a recipe for cheese on toast, this is a fun, pan-cooked version that is worthy of a place in your repertoire. I made it once while on holiday, when I didn't want to heat up the grill, and it has now become a favourite way to make cheese on toast. Have a play with using other veg, too: sliced peppers added along with the onion would be good. I really like this with a sliced head of baby gem lettuce tossed in a simple vinaigrette. My son also loves it as breakfast when we are camping.

SERVES 1 OR 2 AS A SNACK

- 2 thick slices of good-quality bread
- 15g (½oz) butter
- 1 tablespoon olive oil
- 1 small onion, very finely sliced
- pinch of chilli flakes
- 150g (5½oz) Cheddar cheese, or other hard cheese, such as Spenwood, grated

1. You can toast the bread in the frying pan, but I just stick mine in the toaster, being careful to under-toast it slightly, as you don't want it too dry and it will have its moment in the pan.

2. Put the butter and oil in a frying pan over a low heat and tip in the onion. Cook gently for 5–8 minutes or until it has lost its harshness but is not caramelized, otherwise the dish gets too rich and they will start to catch.

3. In the pan, divide the onion into 2 sections, each roughly the shape of your toast, though slightly larger to avoid any dry spots of toast. Add the chilli flakes, followed by the cheese, divided evenly.

4. Add and press the slices of toast gently into each pile of the cheese and onion mix. Move it around a little from side to side, to aid in cheese uptake, then leave until the cheese has melted. Scoop underneath each pile and flip over in a confident manner to warm and gently crisp the naked side of the toast for a moment. Serve at once and enjoy.

TOTAL TIME: 35–45 MINUTES

Potted mushroom pâté

Little jars of pâté are great ready-to-go flavour bombs. Spread it on toast to eat with pickles and a salad as a light meal, or eat the toast with fried or boiled eggs, or use it as a base for cheese on toast. The red cabbage here makes enough for a couple of sittings. Sealed in the fridge, it keeps well for a couple of weeks. You can use the liquid for dressings or seasoning soups or stews, though bear in mind it might change their colour!

MAKES 4 × 250ML (9FL OZ) JARS

- 300g (10½oz) unsalted butter, cubed
- 2 onions, finely sliced
- 1 large rosemary sprig
- 1 large thyme sprig
- 1 leek, cleaned and finely shredded
- 1kg (2lb 4oz) mushrooms (chestnut or portobello are best here), fairly finely chopped
- 6 fat garlic cloves (add a couple more if yours are small), chopped
- 50ml (2fl oz) brandy or cognac
- 1 tablespoon cider vinegar, or other vinegar (optional)
- pinch of sweet paprika
- salt

For the pickled red cabbage (optional)
- 250ml (9fl oz) cider vinegar, or white wine vinegar
- 200ml (7fl oz) water
- 700g (1lb 9oz) red cabbage (about 1 medium), finely shredded

1. Melt 250g (9oz) of the butter in a large pan that will fit all the mushrooms as well. Add the onions, rosemary and thyme with a good pinch of salt. Cook over a medium heat for 8–10 minutes until softened but without too much colour.

2. Add the leek with a further pinch of salt and cook to wilt for 2 minutes. Then follow with the mushrooms and the garlic, increasing the heat a touch to medium-high. You want to get some colour on the mushrooms, but primarily to get rid of their water content.

3. After 6–8 minutes, add the brandy or cognac and bring to a simmer. I find you want to keep this mixture at a gentle simmer for 15–20 minutes to drive off as much water as possible and concentrate the flavours. Go as long as you dare, but just keep stirring so that the mixture doesn't catch.

4. Tip the contents of the pan into a blender and blitz until smooth. Taste and add more salt and the vinegar, if needed. Go slightly past what tastes spot-on because, when chilled, the flavours will be muted. Divide the pâté between sterilized jars (see page 75), or add to 1 big dish. Smooth out the tops and carefully clean any splashes on the edges.

5. Gently melt the remaining butter in a small pan. Add the paprika and a pinch of salt. Stir to combine, then pour the mixture over the pâté to seal and keep fresh. Allow the pâté to cool for 30 minutes, then seal the jars and refrigerate. It keeps for around 2 weeks.

6. If making the pickled red cabbage, bring the vinegar and measured water to a rolling boil in a large saucepan with a few good pinches of salt. Add the cabbage and turn it over a couple of times to coat all the shreds in the liquid. Return to the boil for 1 minute, then remove from the heat. Every few minutes, turn the cabbage again to coat it. When it's cool, transfer to a sealed container and refrigerate.

TOTAL TIME: **40–50 MINUTES**

Georgian spiced spinach & chickpeas

This came about when I was making a curry but had run out of curry powder, so used the Georgian spice *khmeli suneli* instead. It worked so well that we prefer it this way now. But equally, you could go more of an Indian route with spicing, if you have them. *Khmeli suneli* generally contains dill, savory, marigold, coriander and fenugreek among others, giving an earthy complexity.

Eat this with garlic flatbreads such as Spinach Theplas (see page 177), or on top of soft polenta, or with simple boiled rice or potatoes or a fennel salad with dill. If you strain off some of the liquid, it also makes a great filling for pasties or hand pies.

SERVES 4

- 2 tablespoons flavourless oil
- 2 onions, roughly chopped
- 1 leek, cleaned and roughly chopped
- 1 heaped teaspoon fennel seeds, roughly crushed
- 1 teaspoon ground turmeric
- 1 tablespoon khmeli suneli (see recipe introduction), or curry powder
- 500ml (18fl oz) vegetable stock
- 300g (10½oz) frozen spinach, defrosted, or 600g (1lb 5oz) baby leaf spinach, roughly chopped
- 2 × 400g (14oz) cans of chickpeas, or a mixture of carlin peas and chickpeas, drained
- salt

To serve (all optional)
- cooked grains
- sliced fennel and dill dressed in lemon juice
- yogurt
- pickled chillies (for homemade, see page 75), or sliced fresh chillies
- hot sauce (for homemade, see page 75)

1. Place a pan that will fit everything over a medium heat and add the oil, followed by the onions and a good pinch of salt. Cook for 10–12 minutes until the onions are soft and translucent. Add the leek and the spices, stir well and cook for 2–3 minutes, then pour in the stock and bring to a simmer for 5 minutes. Add the spinach and bring back to a bubble for 5 minutes.

2. If you want a finer texture, use a stick blender – or carefully decant into a blender – to break down the spinach and form more of a sauce.

3. Add the chickpeas, or carlin peas and chickpeas, to the veg pan. Cook for 5–10 minutes, then check the seasoning. Serve over grains, with sliced fennel and dill dressed in lemon juice, yogurt, chillies and hot sauce or whatever else floats your boat.

TOTAL TIME: **15–20 MINUTES**

Steamed aubergine with chilli-soy dressing

I love the freshness of this dish: the zingy dressing wakes you up and sends little electric shocks through your taste buds. This is one of those dishes I make when aubergines first appear, as it really celebrates the deliciously silky, sponge-like vegetable. Add crumbled and fried extra-firm tofu if you want to bulk it up a little: just crumble extra-firm tofu into a frying pan with some hot oil, heat through, season with Chinese five spice and serve with the aubergine.

I like to serve these with some simple rice noodles, or I often have leftover grains that provide a landing pad for the aubergines. Alternately, pair them a salad from the Assembly Job chapter.

SERVES 4

- 4 medium-large aubergines
- 25g (1oz) coriander, leaves picked, stalks finely sliced
- cooked rice noodles or grains, or a salad, to serve

For the chilli-soy dressing
- 3 spring onions, finely sliced
- 1–2 red or green chillies, finely chopped
- 1 tablespoon toasted sesame oil (or use chilli oil for more kick)
- 3 tablespoons soy sauce
- 2 tablespoons rice vinegar
- 1 teaspoon honey

1. Set a steamer on the hob, or a large pan that will fit a plate inside with the aubergines on. I like to keep the skin on the aubergines, but peel them if you prefer. Cut each in half. Now you can choose how to cut them: you can score them in a deep cross-hatch, as in the photo, or slice them further into thirds along their length, then into thick batons, cutting each piece into 3 or 4. Pile them into the steamer (you may need a couple of tiers of steaming baskets). If you are using a pan and a large plate, you may have to steam them in a couple of batches. Steam for around 8 minutes until completely tender.

2. Meanwhile, mix all the dressing ingredients together with the coriander stalks.

3. Remove the aubergine from the steamer and dress it with the chilli-soy dressing straight away. Scatter with the coriander leaves and serve with cooked rice noodles or grains, or a salad.

TOTAL TIME: **15 MINUTES**

Sweetcorn fried rice

A staple in our house for any meal of the day, be that a speedy dinner or a family breakfast. This version with corn is lovely and fresh, but you can swap in other ingredients from your veg drawer.

This recipe uses leftover cooked rice, as fried rice is best made using rice that has been pre-cooked and chilled. SERVES 4

- 3–5 tablespoons sunflower oil (quantity depends on whether you're using eggs)
- ½–1 tablespoon soy sauce
- 3 eggs, lightly beaten (optional)
- 300g (10½oz) white or red cabbage, shredded
- 200g (7oz) frozen sweetcorn kernels, defrosted
- 250g (9oz) cold cooked brown short-grain rice
- 1–2 tablespoons rice vinegar, or to taste
- 1 bunch of spring onions, finely sliced
- 15g (½oz) chives, finely chopped (optional)
- sea salt flakes
- togarashi seasoning and/or hot sauce (for homemade hot sauce, see page 75), to serve

1. Heat a large frying pan, or wok if you have one, until it is smoking. Add about 2 tablespoons of the oil to the pan. Mix ½ tablespoon of soy sauce with the eggs, if using, and pour these into the pan. Allow to cook for 15–20 seconds, then start pushing the edges into the centre to allow any uncooked egg to get to the oil. If needed, break the omelette up into sections. Flip it to quickly finish cooking any raw egg mixture. Carefully remove from the pan to a chopping board.

2. Add the remaining oil or, if not using eggs, add 3 tablespoons of oil to the pan, followed by the cabbage with a good pinch of salt. Cook for 7–10 minutes until the cabbage is softened. Add the sweetcorn and continue to cook for another minute. Then follow with the rice and rice vinegar. Turn over to incorporate well, being careful not to break the rice grains too much. After 2–3 minutes everything should be warmed through.

3. Meanwhile, roughly chop the omelette, if using, –1–2cm (½–¾ inch) pieces are fine – then add it to the rice and turn off the heat. Add about three-quarters of the spring onions and the chives, if using.

4. Mix everything well to combine, taste for salt and vinegar levels and add ½ tablespoon of soy or more vinegar to your taste. Serve, scattered with the remaining spring onions and chives, if using, with togarashi and/or hot sauce.

KIDS and OTHER NERVOUS EATERS

This is my experience, and if it is useful to anyone, then that is brilliant.

I find it best to be fairly relaxed around what other people are eating. There is always another meal, another try. Attempting to force people – of any age – to eat, or even to try something, often doesn't yield great success. In fact, it installs a general mistrust in the air. Sometimes you just don't feel like it.

Helping build excitement and fascination with food goes a long way. I let my son get involved in the kitchen from an early age. We bought him a 'learning tower' so that he could stand at the kitchen counter; it has a wooden rail, so he couldn't fall backwards out of it. That allowed him, under our watch, to stir pots of sauce, fry onions or add ingredients to a pan. Simple things, yes, but things that go a long way to igniting a child's interest and, ultimately, willingness to partake in the finished product.

I also bought him a child-friendly Opinel knife for his first birthday for chopping onions, leeks, potatoes, mushrooms, courgettes or whatever wasn't too tough. I just showed him how to cut one side off first and roll the veg on to that flat side to stabilize it for further chopping.

Enabling people to get involved in creating their food is key. Making pasta is a stand-out example of this; a rewarding but easy affair. Whatever the pasta shape is intended to be, my son may go off-piste and create random chopped bits, or just his personally rolled 'trofie'. I keep these separate, then blanch them first, ahead of the main batch, to sit in the sauce and cool slightly. But primarily it is so that he can eat the food that he has made. The first time I did this, I thought it would be quite fun for him to see and eat the pasta that he had rolled. I wasn't expecting the recognition and pride to be so deep. I caught his expression as I put down his plate: he was completely made up. Seeing the results of his work directly was so satisfying, as it should be. Small things that we can brush past are actually really wonderful moments, especially for up-and-coming chefs.

The other big factor that has helped grease the wheels at our table is laying out the components of a meal and allowing everyone to pick what they want, in the proportions they prefer. We place all the elements of a dish on a tray, in piles or small bowls, then set it on the table with a big bowl of any accompanying carbs. That way, if someone doesn't like or isn't sure about an element, they can move past it. This is good for fussy eaters of all ages.

Tasting as you go, a very important part of cooking, also helps to reel in a curious mind. It is fun to taste a sauce or dressing while it is being made, to check whether more seasoning is needed. I like to have the main elements of a dish underway, then take time to make a sauce or dressing to finish everything. This is a good area to allow younger diners to experiment and express themselves, as you can – for the most part – correct it back, if needed. A honey mustard vinaigrette is our go-to, with good oil, cider vinegar, salt and pepper and roughly equal parts of Dijon mustard and honey. My son loves to dip green beans or asparagus into a little pot of this at the table.

Even simpler, a lemon and olive oil dressing for steamed or blanched green veg is always welcome. Along with salt and pepper, your helper can put a good glug of olive oil in a bowl with the juice of a half or whole lemon, give it a whisk to combine and then, when the veg is drained and ready, add it in and toss it well to coat. This is a simple touch that both gets them involved and adds more flavour. (This dressing can also come into play as a little pot on the side.)

Sometimes my son can feel a little overwhelmed when asked what he would like for dinner, as the responsibility can weigh heavily. If that's the case, I'll line up the options – for instance pasta shapes – on the work surface. That way, he can see everything clearly and make a more informed decision. More importantly, it helps him reaffirm his choices with a meal and makes him feel more involved.

All these are methods to consider for anyone for whom eating is not a straightforward act.

IN & OUT OF THE OVEN

Let the oven do some of the heavy lifting in helping to get dinner served. The process of roasting effortlessly brings an extra flavour and texture dimension to all manner of veg, so there's no compromise on taste in these easy dishes, and baking rather than frying is a step in the healthy direction, too. I love that feeling while you wait for the ding of the timer, as you know you're going to be rewarded with something good.

TOTAL TIME: **50 MINUTES – 1 HOUR 5 MINUTES**

Tomato salad with smashed crispy potatoes & mojo verde

When tomatoes are good, I often look for ways to eat them where they remain centre stage. This salad has a lot of elements going on, each ticking its own cravings box: creamy, juicy, crispy, spicy. I love the burst of juicy, sweet, slightly acidic tomatoes against the salty, crispy, fluffy-centred potatoes, all tied together with a deliciously tangy sauce and creamy yielding cheese. If you want to go extra, sub in burrata or, for more tang, a soft goats' cheese. Making up a big platter of this and dropping it in the centre of the table for everyone to help themselves is very satisfying. SERVES 4

- 600g (1lb 5oz) new potatoes
- flavourless oil, for roasting
- 400–500g (14oz–1lb 2oz) ripe tomatoes, ideally a mix of colours, shapes and sizes
- 2 baby gem lettuce, roots trimmed, broken apart into leaves
- 300–400g (10½–14oz) mozzarella cheese, torn into quarters, or bocconcini
- salt

For the mojo verde
(all ingredients to taste)
- 4 tablespoons extra virgin olive oil
- 2 tablespoons sherry vinegar
- 4 garlic cloves
- 50g (1¾oz) coriander
- 1–2 green chillies
- 1 teaspoon ground cumin

1. Preheat the oven to 220°C/200°C fan (425°F), Gas Mark 7. Bring a saucepan of well-salted water to the boil and add the potatoes. Cook until tender when pierced with a knife; 15–20 minutes.

2. Meanwhile, put the *mojo verde* ingredients in a small blender or food processor and blitz until smooth, adding a good pinch of salt. Taste and add more of any ingredient you feel is needed.

3. Drain the potatoes well. Drizzle a couple of tablespoons of oil on to a baking tray. Add the potatoes and crush with a pan or the bottom of a heavy-based glass; they just want to pop and increase the surface area in contact with the tray. Add a further drizzle of oil over the potatoes and put them in the oven. Cook for 30–40 minutes until crisp and golden, flipping them after 25 minutes.

4. As the potatoes are finishing, slice any larger tomatoes thickly. Cut smaller ones in half across their equators.

5. When the potatoes are done, arrange the lettuce on a platter. Top with the warm crispy potatoes sprinkled with salt, followed by the tomatoes and the cheese. Dot over the *mojo verde* and serve.

TOTAL TIME: **1 HOUR – 1 HOUR 10 MINUTES**

Polenta chips with saucy chickpeas

These polenta chips came about when I wanted to bulk up a plate of beans without the mess – and the pan of hot oil – that comes with making chips. The polenta can be made and set ahead, either during the day or the night before, or it will sit happily for a couple of days in the fridge. Cut the chips however you please: little cubes to simulate home fries is fun, or thinner strips that get a bit more crunchy. Or, if you are in a rush, just make the polenta a little wetter and serve it soft, with the chickpeas over the top. SERVES 4

- olive oil, for greasing and frying
- 800ml (1⅓ pints) vegetable stock
- 1 tablespoon dried oregano
- 200g (7oz) quick-cook polenta
- 2 small onions, roughly chopped
- 3 garlic cloves, sliced
- 2 peppers (any colour), cored, deseeded and roughly chopped
- 1 tablespoon hot paprika
- 400g (14oz) can of plum tomatoes
- 2 × 400g (14oz) cans of chickpeas, or 1 large (700g/1lb 9oz) jar
- salt
- grated hard cheese, such as Spenwood, to serve (optional)

For the green sauce
- 25g (1oz) parsley, leaves picked and finely chopped
- 2 tablespoons drained capers, chopped
- 6–8 cornichons, finely chopped
- 2–3 tablespoons red wine vinegar (or other vinegar works fine), plus more to taste

1. Line a small baking tray with nonstick baking paper and rub lightly with oil all over.

2. Bring the stock to a bubble with the oregano in a saucepan. Rain in the polenta while stirring with a whisk. Cook out over a medium–low heat for 3–5 minutes, whisking all the while. Pour into the prepared baking tray and put in the fridge to chill and set; 15–30 minutes should be fine.

3. Meanwhile, preheat the oven to 220°C/200°C fan (425°F), Gas Mark 7. Put a baking tray inside to heat up.

4. Put 2–3 tablespoons of oil in a frying pan over a medium heat. Follow with the onions and a good pinch of salt and cook until beginning to soften; 6–8 minutes. Add the garlic, peppers and paprika and cook for 2–3 minutes, then add the canned tomatoes with their juice, crushing up the tomatoes a little with your wooden spoon. Rinse out the tomato can with about half its volume of water and add to the pan, followed by the chickpeas and their juice. Bring to a simmer and cook for 10–15 minutes.

5. Cut the polenta into chunky (or however you want; see recipe introduction) chips and dress them lightly with oil. Carefully remove the hot baking tray from the oven and space the polenta chips out evenly on it. Bake in the oven for 20–25 minutes, turning after 15 minutes, until crisp.

6. Meanwhile, mix all the green sauce ingredients together. Taste and add salt and more vinegar, if needed.

7. Serve the chickpeas with the polenta chips on top, scattered with grated cheese, if you like, and the green sauce on the side.

IN & OUT OF THE OVEN

TOTAL TIME: 30-40 MINUTES

Roast hispi with toasted seeds & crumbled chestnuts

Charred hispi cabbage has been on many a plate in our house and it stands up really well to hard cooking, so you could barbecue the wedges, if you've got a barbecue fired up. Maybe drop the chestnuts in the warmer months and sub in pomegranate seeds. Simply served with rice, pasta or flatbreads and a dollop of yogurt, this is a lovely dish, with lots of textures and flavours going on.
SERVES 4

- 2 hispi cabbages (or white cabbages also work fine), quartered
- olive oil, for rubbing and toasting
- 50g (1¾oz) pumpkin seeds
- 50g (1¾oz) sunflower seeds
- 1 tablespoon cumin seeds
- 200g (7oz) cooked chestnuts, crumbled
- finely grated zest and juice of 1 lemon
- 300g (10½oz) yogurt
- 10g (¼oz) dill, sprigs picked and finely chopped
- 10g (¼oz) coriander, leaves picked, stalks finely chopped
- 15g (½oz) chives, finely chopped
- sea salt flakes and black pepper

1. Preheat the oven to 220°C/200°C fan (425°F), Gas Mark 7. Rub the quarters of cabbage with oil and sprinkle with sea salt flakes. Spread out evenly on a baking tray and put in the oven to roast for 25–35 minutes, rotating the tray and flipping the cabbage sections after 20 minutes.

2. Meanwhile, put the pumpkin and sunflower seeds in a small frying pan with 2 tablespoons of oil and toast gently over a medium–low heat until golden and fragrant – 2–3 minutes should do; don't go too dark – stirring in the cumin seeds 30 seconds before you turn off the heat. Allow to sit for a couple of minutes, then mix in the cooked chestnuts with a pinch of sea salt flakes and a few good grinds of black pepper.

3. Mix the lemon zest and juice, a pinch of salt and the yogurt together in a separate bowl. Stir in the dill, coriander and half the chives.

4. Spread the yogurt-herb mixture on to a plate or serving platter, top with the hispi, then spoon over the chestnut–seed mix. Finish with the remaining chives and serve.

IN & OUT OF THE OVEN

TOTAL TIME: 35–45 MINUTES

Baked mushroom parmigiana

I like these with simple boiled new potatoes and a green salad, or in a sandwich (peak satisfaction). After the initial breadcrumbing is done, the oven does the work here; you just need a carb on the side. Decadent midweek eating. SERVES 4

- olive oil, for roasting
- 50g (1¾oz) hard cheese, such as Spenwood (other hard sheep's or cows' cheeses work fine too), coarsely grated
- 1 tablespoon dried oregano
- 200g (7oz) breadcrumbs, or roughly torn day-old bread
- 4 eggs, lightly beaten
- 500g (1lb 2oz) oyster mushrooms
- 100g (3½oz) plain flour
- salt and black pepper
- extra virgin olive oil, to serve (optional)

For the tomato sauce
- 2 tablespoons olive oil
- 5 garlic cloves, sliced
- 15g (½oz) basil, leaves picked, stalks finely chopped
- 2 × 400g (14oz) cans of plum tomatoes
- 100ml (3½fl oz) white wine (optional)

1. Preheat the oven to 240°C/220°C fan (475°F), Gas Mark 9. Brush a large baking tray with olive oil.

2. Mix the cheese and oregano together with the breadcrumbs in a dish. Put the eggs in a second dish and the flour, seasoned with salt and pepper, in a third.

3. Dust the mushrooms with flour to coat (it doesn't cling exceptionally well, but will help build a crust). Dunk the mushrooms into the egg and then the breadcrumb mixture, placing them on the prepared baking tray as you go. Don't crowd them; use a second tray if needed. Drizzle the mushrooms with olive oil and bake in the oven for 15–20 minutes, then flip them, as well as rotating the trays in the oven. Cook for a further 10–15 minutes until golden and crisp but not dried out.

4. Meanwhile, make the tomato sauce. Heat the oil in a large frying pan over a medium heat. Add the garlic and stir for a minute, then follow with the basil stalks and the canned tomatoes, crushing the tomatoes with a wooden spoon or masher. Rinse out the tomato cans with about one-quarter their volume of water and pour into the pan, along with the wine, if using. Bring to a simmer to reduce and thicken the sauce, and just marry the ingredients. It shouldn't be watery, so increase the heat if needed.

5. Remove the mushrooms from the oven to a wire rack to cool for a couple of minutes, then transfer to serving plates, dotting the tomato sauce in between the mushrooms and scattering over the basil leaves with a few twists of black pepper. A drizzle of extra virgin olive oil is also welcome.

TOTAL TIME: **35–40 MINUTES**

Squash & feta frittata

I've really taken to making solo versions of this for myself, as it's speedy and tasty. Cooking the cubes of squash in the pan concentrates the flavours, as well as cutting down on mess. As with the majority of the recipes in this book, have a play. If you have ends of veg, finely chop them and add them in, or I often throw in 200g (7oz) of petits pois straight from the freezer. You can also add ends of cheese from the fridge, cubed up; I do like little nuggets of cheese rather than the grated version, as they help create pockets of flavour.

The photo is of a frittata for two, as the recipe is easily scaleable both up and down. Serve with green veg or a salad, or just on its own. SERVES 4

- 2–3 tablespoons olive oil
- 2 red onions, chopped
- 800g (1lb 12oz) prepared butternut squash, or other squash or pumpkin, cut into rough 1cm (½ inch) cubes
- 200ml (7fl oz) water
- 10g (¼oz) parsley, finely chopped
- 8 eggs, lightly beaten
- 200g (7oz) feta cheese, cut into 1cm (½ inch) cubes
- salt and black pepper

1. Preheat the oven to 200°C/180°C fan (400°F), Gas Mark 6.

2. Set a 30cm (12 inch) ovenproof frying pan over a medium–low heat. Heat the oil and add the onions with a good pinch of salt. Cook for 5 minutes, then increase the heat to medium and add the squash or pumpkin and measured water. Cook for 8–10 minutes until the squash is tender, topping up the water if you think it needs it, but bearing in mind that the water needs to completely evaporate before the next step.

3. Evenly disperse the onion-squash/pumpkin mixture over the base of the frying pan. Add a small pinch of salt to season the squash/pumpkin and reduce the heat back to medium–low. Beat the parsley into the eggs in a bowl, season with salt and black pepper, then gently pour the eggs into the pan. Add the feta cubes, sprinkling them evenly across the pan. Cook for 1–2 minutes to set the bottom of the frittata.

4. Put the pan in the oven to cook the frittata through for 15–20 minutes until golden and lightly puffed up. Remove from the oven carefully, as the handle will be very hot, and serve.

TOTAL TIME: 35–40 MINUTES

Brothy shallots & butter beans with a herb crust

This is a pretty no-nonsense dish to bring together. Adding crème fraîche is a nice way to introduce a little opulence, but it isn't necessary if you want a lighter-on-its-feet option. Don't go too fine with the breadcrumbs, as texture is very welcome here. I really like this as is, or simply with boiled new potatoes. SERVES 4

- 25g (1oz) parsley
- 6 tablespoons olive oil
- 300g (10½oz) sourdough bread, cut into rough cubes
- finely grated zest of 1 lemon (optional)
- 1–1.2kg (2lb 4oz–2lb 10oz) banana shallots, halved lengthways
- 3 garlic cloves, sliced
- 1 litre (1¾ pints) stock, or 2 stock cubes dissolved in 1 litre (1¾ pints) hot water
- 2 × 400g (14oz) cans of butter beans, drained
- 100g (3½oz) crème fraîche (optional)
- 1–2 tablespoons cider vinegar, or more to taste
- sea salt flakes and black pepper

1. Preheat the oven to 220°C/200°C fan (425°F), Gas Mark 7.

2. Put the parsley and 4 tablespoons of the oil in a food processor. Equally, finely chopping the parsley by hand works. Toss in the bread with a good pinch of salt, along with the lemon zest, if using, and blitz until a rough crumb is achieved. Set aside.

3. In an ovenproof pan that will fit everything, to save on washing-up (otherwise use a separate oven dish), heat the remaining 2 tablespoons of oil over a medium heat. Add the shallots, cut side down, and cook for 5 minutes. Give them a stir, add the garlic and cook for 2 minutes, then follow with the stock and beans. Bring to a simmer and allow the broth to reduce slightly for 7–10 minutes until saucy but not too watery. Stir in the crème fraîche at this point, if using, as well as the vinegar; taste and add more vinegar if you like.

4. Decant the shallots and butter beans to an oven dish, or stay with the pan you've been using if it's ovenproof. Add the breadcrumbs in an even layer and place in the oven for 15–20 minutes to get them crispy and golden. Remove and serve.

IN & OUT OF THE OVEN

TOTAL TIME: **50-55 MINUTES**

Grain & veg traybake salad

If you have time – and you have remembered – it is really worth soaking the grains overnight, or through the day; just chuck them in a mixing bowl of water with 1½ tablespoons of lemon juice or vinegar as you are going out in the morning. Soaking them means they are faster to cook, the grains are more tender and their nutrients can be more available to your body to digest. SERVES 4

- 300g (10½oz) wheat berries, pearled barley, oat groats or your favoured grain, ideally soaked for at least 6 hours (see recipe introduction and page 167)
- 250g (9oz) banana shallots, or small onions (about 5), halved lengthways
- 200g (7oz) carrots, cut into 1–2cm (½–¾ inch) chunks diagonally
- 1 fennel bulb, quartered
- olive oil, for roasting and dressing
- 1 apple, cored and chopped into 1cm (½ inch) cubes
- finely grated zest and juice of 1 lemon
- 2 celery sticks, finely chopped, or 1 kohlrabi, peeled and finely chopped
- 3 spring onions, finely sliced
- 50g (1¾oz) soft herbs, such as mint, dill, coriander, parsley, tarragon, chervil or even basil, roughly chopped
- salt and black pepper

1. Preheat the oven to 220°C/200°C (425°F), Gas Mark 7.

2. If you soaked the grains, drain them and, either way, tip them into a saucepan of well-salted boiling water. Cook until tender: non-soaked grains take 30–40 minutes; soaked should take more like 15–20 minutes. Drain and leave to cool slightly.

3. Meanwhile, toss the shallots, carrots and fennel in a couple tablespoons of oil and place in a baking tray. Add a pinch of salt and roast until tender; 25–35 minutes. Remove from the oven to cool.

4. In a bowl, dress the apple in the lemon juice to stop it from discolouring. Add the celery or kohlrabi, spring onions, lemon zest and herbs with a decent pinch of salt.

5. When the veg is tender and cool enough to handle, chop through it roughly. Add the herb mix and the slightly cooled grains. Check the seasoning and add olive oil, salt and pepper to taste, then serve.

TOTAL TIME: **1 HOUR 10 MINUTES – 1 HOUR 25 MINUTES**

Kraut-loaded baked potatoes

I hadn't thought of anything to make for dinner, so I just threw some potatoes in the oven and went and did the school run. When I got back, I discovered there weren't any trusty baked potato toppings either, so I had to think outside the box, using bits that were in the fridge… and these guys were born. When I tell my family I'm making them now, the news is met with much glee. I suppose they have some footing in Ukrainian flavours (my wife is Ukrainian), so you could think of using feta instead of Cheddar, to lean more into that. Wherever they are from, they are tasty and filling, though quite light because of all the veg.

Putting them back in the oven after filling them melts the cheese properly, yes, but is mainly to take the raw edge off the onion. So, if you want to be even speedier, cook the onion for a few minutes while the potatoes are in the oven. Dare I suggest, you could even cook it for a long time and caramelize it. SERVES 4

1. Preheat the oven to 220°C/200°C fan (425°F), Gas Mark 7. Add the potatoes and cook until a knife easily pierces the flesh; around 45 minutes – 1 hour.

2. Remove the potatoes from the oven, leaving the oven on, and slice them in half – I use a clean tea towel to help with this, as they're hot! – then scoop the flesh into a mixing bowl. You don't have to be too diligent, as you want to leave some flesh in the skins to help the potatoes keep their shape. Mix the remaining ingredients, except the oil and one-quarter of the cheese, into the potato flesh. Stuff the mixture back into the potato skins, top with the remaining cheese and drizzle with oil.

3. Return the potatoes to the oven for another 15 minutes until piping hot and the cheese has melted, then serve with hot sauce, if liked.

- 1kg (2lb 4oz) baking potatoes, scrubbed
- 350g (12oz) sauerkraut
- 200g (7oz) Cheddar cheese, or smoked cheese, grated
- 1 onion, finely sliced
- 250g (9oz) white cabbage, shredded
- 15g (½oz) dill, finely chopped
- 2–3 sliced jalapeños (other chillies are fine, too)
- olive oil, for drizzling
- hot sauce, to serve (optional; for homemade, see page 75)

TOTAL TIME: **30–35 MINUTES**

Baked rice with chickpeas

I love this as a back-up, quick-cook rice dish that can be a main course or a side dish, depending on how you serve it. It works a treat with mushroom stock, and you can make your own by adding a heaped tablespoon of mushroom powder to 600ml (20fl oz) of boiling water. You can make the powder by blitzing up dried mushrooms in a spice blender, or even in a standard blender. You need 750ml (1¹⁄₃ pints) liquid in totaly (from the chickpea juice, wine and stock); generally I get 300ml (½ pint) juice from 2 cans of chickpeas. SERVES 4

- 2–3 tablespoons olive oil
- 1 onion, finely chopped
- 2 garlic cloves, sliced
- 1–2 tablespoons paprika (a mix of sweet and smoked is good, if possible)
- 250g (9oz) paella rice, or risotto rice
- 2 × 400g (14oz) cans of chickpeas, or carlin peas, or 1 large (700g/1lb 9oz) jar
- 150ml (¼ pint) white wine, or cider
- 300ml (½ pint) hot vegetable stock, or mushroom stock (see recipe introduction)
- salt

1. Preheat the oven to 200°C/180°C fan (400°F), Gas Mark 6.

2. In a wide, high-sided ovenproof pan – I use a 24cm (9½ inch) sauté pan – heat the oil over a medium heat. Add the onion and a pinch of salt, then reduce the heat to medium–low and cook the onion for 8–10 minutes until soft and translucent. Add the garlic with the paprika and cook for a minute, then follow with the rice and chickpeas or carlin peas, juice and all. Mix well, but don't over-stir.

3. Pour in the wine or cider and bring to a simmer, trying not to stir the rice too much. Add the hot stock, return to a simmer for 1 minute, then transfer the pan to the oven.

4. Cook the rice for 10 minutes, then turn the pan 180 degrees and cook for a further 6–8 minutes until the liquid has been absorbed. Serve warm. I like to put the pan in the centre of the table for everyone to help themselves, but just be careful: it is hot!

TOTAL TIME: **30–35 MINUTES**

Baked rice with peas

My wife requested rice and peas one night, so I shuffled the recipe opposite around to satisfy her request. It turned out great. The 'peas' are actually kidney beans, as in the classic Jamaican dish. We ate this with a cucumber, gherkin and sauerkraut salad: brilliant early summer eating. I wanted to include it in the book, along with the preceding recipe, to illustrate how shifting ingredients around a little can take you in a very satisfying direction, as well as to reinforce my mantra: use what you have to hand. In the initial recipe, I used Lebanese seven spice, as that's what I had. While, of course, that isn't the traditional way, I like that it gets close and satisfies the craving. Ferments or a fresh salad are good alongside. SERVES 4

- 2–3 tablespoons flavourless oil
- 1 onion, finely chopped
- 2 garlic cloves, sliced
- 2 thyme sprigs, leaves picked
- ½ teaspoon allspice, or Lebanese 7 spice
- 250g (9oz) paella rice, or risotto rice
- 2 × 400g (14oz) cans of red kidney beans, or 1 large (700g/1lb 9oz) jar, drained and rinsed
- 400g (14oz) can of coconut milk
- 350ml (12oz) hot vegetable stock, or mushroom stock (see recipe introduction, opposite)
- 1 Scotch Bonnet, or other chilli, whole
- salt

1. Preheat the oven to 200°C/180°C fan (400°F), Gas Mark 6.

2. In a wide, high-sided ovenproof pan – I use a 24cm (9½ inch) sauté pan – heat the oil over a medium heat. Add the onion and a pinch of salt, then reduce the heat to medium–low and cook the onion for 8–10 minutes until soft and translucent. Add the garlic, thyme and allspice or 7 spice and cook for a minute, then follow with the rice and beans. Mix well to coat everything in the oil.

3. Add the coconut milk, hot stock and chilli. Bring to a simmer for 2 minutes, trying not to stir the rice too much, then transfer the pan to the oven.

4. Cook the rice for 10 minutes, then turn the pan 180 degrees and cook for a further 6–8 minutes until the liquid has been absorbed. Serve warm, as opposite.

IN & OUT OF THE OVEN

TOTAL TIME: **40–50 MINUTES**

Oven-baked onion bhajis

Here you get the satisfaction of an onion bhaji but without the oil and frying. This is fairly low input and all the magic happens in the oven. Slicing onions is probably my favourite kitchen task; I used to volunteer to slice whole sacks. If that isn't you, use a machine to speed things up. MAKES 16

- 100g (3½oz) gram (chickpea) flour
- 50g (1¾oz) cornflour
- ½ teaspoon baking powder
- 1 tablespoon fennel seeds
- 1 tablespoon cumin seeds
- 1 tablespoon nigella seeds
- 1 teaspoon Kashmiri chilli powder (optional)
- 4 large onions, or 8 regular onions, finely sliced
- flavourless oil, for greasing and drizzling

For the sauce
- 150g (5½oz) yogurt
- 10g (¼oz) mint, leaves picked and shredded, plus more (optional), roughly chopped, to garnish
- salt

1. Preheat the oven to 220°C/200°C fan (425°F), Gas Mark 7. Place a couple of baking trays in the oven to warm through 5 minutes ahead of putting the fritters in the oven.

2. Mix the dry ingredients together in a large mixing bowl. Add the sliced onions and toss to combine well, then splash in a little water at a time to just help a batter form around the onions, but not too loose; 3–4 tablespoons should be enough.

3. Remove the trays from the oven and brush or drizzle them with a little oil. Grab little piles of onion mix, dot on to the oiled trays and pat them down lightly, then drizzle each with a little more oil.

4. Place the bhajis in the oven for 30–40 minutes until crisp and golden, turning the trays 180 degrees after 25 minutes.

5. To make the sauce, mix the yogurt with the shredded mint and a pinch of salt.

6. Remove the onion bhajis from the oven and serve, scattered with chopped mint, if you like, with the sauce.

TOTAL TIME: 35-45 MINUTES

Baked Cheddar semolina with puttanesca sauce

Originally, this was to be a Roman gnocchi-style recipe, but in the spirit of midweek cookery, which needs speed, I figured we'd forgo shaping the semolina. Instead, dolloping the semolina mixture on the sauce and melting over cheese to get crispy edges seemed rather appealing. By all means, smooth it out, or shape it more neatly, but for me the scraggly edges are where it's at. That and the wonderful rich briny acidic punch of the sauce beneath. Adding a tin or 2 of drained chickpeas or beans would stretch this recipe to serve 6. SERVES 4 WELL

- 3 tablespoons olive oil
- 3 onions, roughly chopped
- 2 × 400g (14oz) cans of plum tomatoes
- 5 garlic cloves, roughly sliced
- 200g (7oz) kalamata or other black olives, or mixed olives, pitted and torn in half
- 3 tablespoons drained capers
- 15g (½oz) parsley, leaves picked and finely chopped
- 1-2 tablespoons red wine vinegar, to taste
- salt and black pepper

For the semolina
- 500ml (18fl oz) vegetable stock
- 500ml (18fl oz) whole milk
- 250g (9oz) semolina
- 250g (9oz) cheese (Cheddar is good, but try other similar hard cheese), grated

1. Preheat the oven to 220°C/200°C fan (425°F), Gas Mark 7.

2. Heat the oil in a frying pan over a medium heat. Add the onions and soften for 10-12 minutes. Add the canned tomatoes and garlic, crushing up the tomatoes with a wooden spoon or a masher. Rinse out the tomato cans with about one-third their volume of water and add to the pot. Bring to a simmer and bubble away for 5-7 minutes to reduce slightly.

3. Meanwhile, make the semolina. Bring the stock and milk to a simmer in a saucepan. Add a good couple of pinches of salt and then rain in the semolina, whisking as you go. Cook for 3-4 minutes until thick, then stir through 200g (7oz) of the cheese, check the seasoning and add more if needed.

4. Turn on the grill-plus-oven setting of the oven. Stir the olives, capers, parsley and vinegar to taste through the tomato sauce, check the seasoning, then pour it into a baking dish.

5. Dollop over the semolina evenly and scatter the rest of the cheese on top. Place under the oven grill, close the door and cook until golden and melted, bubbling and crispy at the edges; 10-15 minutes should be good. Serve immediately.

IN & OUT OF THE OVEN

TOTAL TIME: **40-50 MINUTES**

Freeform mushroom lasagne

'Lasagne' is a loose term here, but you get the same satisfaction from this dish as you would from a more traditional version. While I really enjoy the mega-project of constructing a classic lasagne, I appreciate that it isn't an everyday dish, and this method gets pretty close in a fraction of the time.

I wanted to make this one-pot, but I failed because it really does benefit from the bechamel. However, if you are in a rush, beat a tub of ricotta with a little milk and pour that over instead, then grate over the cheese. If using dried pasta, use 250g (9oz) and blanch it for 3-5 minutes until floppy but not cooked through, then add directly to the mushroom mix. SERVES 4

- 3-4 tablespoons olive oil
- 1 onion, finely chopped
- 1 celery stick, finely chopped
- 1 carrot, finely chopped
- 60g (2¼oz) flour
- 60g (2¼oz) unsalted butter
- 1 bay leaf
- 600ml (20fl oz) whole milk
- 100g (3½oz) hard cheese, such as Spenwood, grated, plus more to serve
- 600g (1lb 5oz) mixed mushrooms, roughly chopped
- 3 garlic cloves, sliced
- 100ml (3½fl oz) white wine
- 400g (14oz) can of plum tomatoes
- 1 tablespoon dried oregano
- 300g (10½oz) fresh lasagne sheets, torn into large chunks (or see recipe introduction)
- salt and black pepper

1. In a large shallow ovenproof pan that will fit everything, heat the oil over a medium heat, then add the onion, celery and carrot with a pinch of salt. Cook, stirring occasionally, for 10-12 minutes until soft.

2. Meanwhile, toast the flour in a separate saucepan over a medium heat, stirring with a whisk until golden. Melt in the butter to form a wet sand consistency. Add the bay leaf, then pour in the milk in 4 batches, whisking each batch in completely before adding the next. When you have a smooth sauce that is the consistency of thick cream, turn off the heat and stir in the cheese. Check the seasoning and add salt and pepper to taste.

3. Preheat the oven to 220°C/200°C fan (425°F), Gas Mark 7.

4. Add the mushrooms to the onion mixture and cook for 5-7 minutes until they release their moisture and reduce in size, adding the garlic for the final minute. Pour in the wine and bring to a bubble, then add the canned tomatoes, crushing them with a wooden spoon. Now fill the tomato can with water and add to the pan, along with the oregano, then return to a bubble for 5 minutes. The mixture needs to be fairly wet; a little evaporation is good to get all the flavours to begin to marry, but it shouldn't be too dry, as the pasta will absorb a lot of liquid.

5. Add the pasta and stir to immerse it in the sauce. Remove the bay leaf from the bechamel, pour this over the saucy pasta and put the pan in the oven. Bake for 15-20 minutes until golden on top and bubbling. Serve with more cheese alongside.

TOTAL TIME: 1 HOUR 10 MINUTES – 1 HOUR 25 MINUTES, PLUS SOAKING, FOR DRIED BEANS; 40–45 MINUTES FOR CANNED BEANS

Roast onion soup with butter beans & olive-rosemary croutons

So quick and easy to make, this comes together in minutes, especially if you make the croutons ahead of time and keep them in an airtight container (though that's dangerous, as I use them to snack on, so I have to make them again anyway). With just enough deepness from the roasted onions and lovely crunchy big croutons, this is simple and soul-warming. SERVES 4

- 1.2kg (2lb 10oz) onions, halved
- 1 garlic bulb, halved across its equator
- 2–3 thyme sprigs
- 8 tablespoons olive oil
- 300g (10½oz) sourdough (about 4 thick slices), cut or torn into rough 2cm (¾ inch) chunks
- 3 rosemary sprigs, leaves picked and roughly chopped
- 75g (2¾oz) kalamata or other black olives, pitted and chopped
- 1.5 litres (2¾ pints) hot vegetable stock
- 250g (9oz) dried butter beans (or haricot, cannellini or any white beans really), soaked overnight or for 8 hours, cooked and drained (see pages 166–7), or 2 × 400g (14oz) cans, drained
- salt

1. Preheat the oven to 220°C/200°C fan (425°F), Gas Mark 7. Place a large oven tray inside to heat.

2. Put the onions, garlic and thyme in a separate deep-sided roasting tray with 4 tablespoons of the olive oil and a good pinch of salt, then toss well to coat evenly. Roast for 25–35 minutes until the onions are collapsing and starting to caramelize.

3. Meanwhile, toss the bread in the remaining 4 tablespoons of oil and a good pinch of salt in a large mixing bowl to coat well. Remove the large tray from the oven and spread out the oiled bread evenly. Return the tray to the oven for 15 minutes, then give the tray a shake, rotate it 180 degrees and cook for a further 10 minutes. Add the rosemary and olives, turn them over to incorporate with the bread cubes, then cook for a final 5 minutes.

4. When the onions are cooked, squeeze the garlic cloves from their skins into the tray and stir in the stock. Then either in a blender or with a stick blender, blitz until smooth, or leave the soup more brothy, as you prefer. Stir in the beans. Serve the soup with the olive-crouton mixture piled into a bowl, for everyone to add on top of their own soup.

IN & OUT OF THE OVEN

TOTAL TIME: **45 MINUTES**

Squash & blue cheese risotto with toasted pecans & crispy sage

This is my trusty, go-to risotto recipe. Essentially you are making a white base, adding flavour and colour only at the final stages. If you are preparing it ahead, you can make the risotto up to the point of the rice being al dente, then cool. When you're ready to eat, reheat with a splash of water and stir in the roasted veg.

I try not to make this too rich, but do add more hard cheese if you like. Using the Stilton means you actually don't need that much, as the flavour is strong and you don't want it to overpower the other flavours. SERVES 4

- 1 butternut squash or pumpkin, about 650g (1lb 7oz)
- 80g (2¾oz) pecans
- olive oil, for cooking
- 2 small onions, finely chopped
- 2 celery sticks, finely chopped
- 2 garlic cloves, finely sliced
- 75g (2¾oz) butter
- 15g (½oz) sage
- 300g (10½oz) risotto rice
- 200ml (7fl oz) white wine
- 1 litre (1¾ pints) hot vegetable stock
- 50g (1¾oz) hard cheese, such as Spenwood, grated
- 125–200g (4½–7oz) Stilton, or other blue cheese, crumbled
- pinch of chilli flakes (optional)
- salt
- extra virgin olive oil, to serve

1. Preheat the oven to 220°C/200°C fan (425°F), Gas Mark 7.

2. Peel and deseed the squash or pumpkin, then cut into 1–2cm (½–¾ inch) cubes. Toss with olive oil and a good pinch of salt. Place on a baking tray and roast for 25–35 minutes until tender and caramelized at the edges. Tip the pecans on to a small baking tray and toast them in the oven for 6–8 minutes until fragrant. It's better to err on the side of undercooked here, as they can burn quickly.

3. Meanwhile, add 2–3 tablespoons of olive oil to a sauté pan over a medium–low heat and add the onions, celery, garlic and 50g (1¾oz) of the butter. Cook this gently for about 15 minutes; you are looking for very soft veg without colour.

4. Heat a couple of tablespoons of oil in a small frying pan over a medium heat, then add the sage and a pinch of salt. Cook, stirring, until the oil mostly stops bubbling and the leaves become rigid. Remove the leaves from the heat and place on a plate lined with kitchen paper, to soak up the excess oil.

5. Add the rice to the onion pan, increase the heat to medium–high and toast it for 3 minutes. When it is fragrant, add the wine. Allow this to be absorbed, then start adding the hot stock, 2 ladles at a time. Allow the liquid to be absorbed, stirring fairly constantly, before adding the next batch. Once all the stock is in, beat in the remaining butter.

6. Stir in the squash or pumpkin and check the seasoning, adding the grated cheese. Divide between warmed bowls and dot over as much blue cheese as you like. Roughly break up the pecans and scatter over, followed by the crispy sage and chilli flakes, if using. Drizzle with extra virgin olive oil and serve.

TOTAL TIME: 35–45 MINUTES

Filo baked feta with roast red pepper & cucumber salad

I really enjoy adding a different dimension to feta, and here the crispy shards of pastry add texture to the salty soft sheep's cheese. It's lovely and fresh. You can add beans or grains to bulk this out to be a more robust dish, if needed (as in the photo). I like to use kidney beans; 1 tin, drained and added to the salad, will do nicely. SERVES 4

- 1–2 tablespoons olive oil, or flavourless oil, plus more for the pastry
- 3 red peppers
- 8 sheets of filo pastry, or brik pastry
- 2 × 200g (7oz) blocks of feta cheese, each halved lengthways
- 1 large cucumber, or 4 small Lebanese cucumbers
- 1 red onion, finely sliced
- 40g (1½oz) drained capers
- 15g (½oz) mint, leaves picked and roughly chopped (optional)
- 2–3 tablespoons sherry vinegar, or red or white wine vinegar, to taste
- 4–6 tablespoons extra virgin olive oil, to taste
- salt and black pepper

1. Preheat the oven to 220°C/200°C fan (425°F), Gas Mark 7. Rub the olive or flavourless oil on the peppers, put them on a baking tray and roast until collapsing; this will take 20–30 minutes. Once done, place the peppers in a covered mixing bowl to steam; this will help release the skins from the flesh.

2. Meanwhile, brush a sheet of pastry lightly with oil. Place a block of the feta in the middle, with a long side facing you. Fold the pastry closest to you up and over the feta. Then fold in the left and right sides. Finally, fold the feta block away from you until the pastry is fully encasing it. Oil a second sheet of pastry and wrap the block again. Repeat to assemble 4 feta parcels, placing them on a baking tray as they're completed.

3. Bake the parcels for 25–35 minutes until golden and crisp, rotating the tray 180 degrees halfway through the cooking time.

4. Once the peppers are cool enough to handle, peel the skins from the flesh, remove the seeds and stalks and cut or pull the flesh into strips. Place the strips in a bowl.

5. Cut diagonal chunks from the cucumber(s), rotating a quarter turn with each cut. Add the chunks to the red pepper, with the onion, capers and mint, if using. Add the vinegar and extra virgin olive oil to taste. Season with salt and black pepper. Serve the feta parcels with the salad alongside.

TOTAL TIME: **35-40 MINUTES**

Fried potato omelette with blue cheese

I ordered this at a restaurant in France a few years back, where omelette was the veggie main option, which I'm okay with... especially, in this case, as what was served was brilliant. Sautéed potatoes, crisp and golden, encased in a fluffy omelette cooked over a high heat with rather a lot of molten cheese. If I remember correctly, I had a choice of cheeses, and the blue stood out as a funkier option, but you do you and choose your favoured cheese, just remembering that one that melts well is key. I have made this recipe as a sharing-sized omelette, but it's simple to scale down for a solo serving, as shown in the photo. SERVES 4

- 800g (1lb 12oz) new potatoes
- 25g (1oz) unsalted butter
- 2 tablespoons olive oil
- 8 eggs
- 200g (7oz) blue cheese, broken into 1–2cm (½–¾ inch) pieces, or more if you wish
- salt
- 7g (¼oz) chives, finely chopped

1. Bring a saucepan of well-salted water to the boil and add the potatoes. Cook until tender when pierced with a knife; 15–20 minutes. Drain and allow to steam-dry briefly, then slice into coins 1cm (½ inch) thick.

2. Preheat the oven to 200°C/180°C fan (400°F), Gas Mark 6.

3. Set an ovenproof frying pan over a medium heat and add the butter and oil, then carefully add the potatoes. Cook until golden on the first side – 3–4 minutes should do it – then flip the potatoes and repeat on the other side.

4. Meanwhile, lightly beat the eggs in a bowl with a good pinch of salt.

5. Pour the eggs into the frying pan, making sure that they are evenly distributed, then dot over the cheese. Cook for a minute on the hob, then transfer to the oven.

6. Once the eggs are set and cooked through, which should take 4–5 minutes, you are ready to serve. Carefully remove the pan from the oven with a cloth, as the handle will be very hot. Top with the chives and serve.

IN & OUT OF THE OVEN

TOTAL TIME: 55 MINUTES – 1 HOUR

Baked buffalo cauliflower

This is a killer combo, either piled into a flatbread – try my Homemade Tortillas (see page 72) – or eaten with rice or other grains. The salad can be all cabbage, if that's what you have, or add in other greens or herbs if you like. SERVES 4

1. Preheat the oven to 230°C/210°C fan (450°F), Gas Mark 8. Line 1 or 2 large baking sheets with nonstick baking paper.

2. Mix the flours in a mixing bowl with the garlic, paprika and salt, then gradually whisk in the olive oil and measured water to make a thick batter that is loose enough to coat without being runny (you may not need all the water). Add the cauliflower slices to the bowl and toss well to coat evenly. Remove each section of cauliflower carefully, ideally with tongs, allowing any major excess of batter to fall off, then swiftly place on the prepared sheet(s), allowing for the cauliflower to be spaced out enough so that each piece crisps up.

3. Slide the baking sheet(s) into the oven and bake the cauliflower for 25 minutes, then flip the pieces over and continue to bake for 20–25 minutes until tender when pierced with a knife and crisp.

4. Meanwhile, combine all the salad ingredients in a bowl, then taste and add more lemon juice if needed.

5. Serve the cauliflower alongside the salad, with cooked grains and some hot sauce, if liked.

- 75g (2¾oz) plain flour
- 25g (1oz) cornflour, or more plain flour
- 2 teaspoons garlic powder, or 2 garlic cloves, finely grated
- 1 tablespoon smoked paprika
- 1 teaspoon fine sea salt
- 2 tablespoons olive oil
- 75–100ml (2½–3½fl oz) water
- 2 cauliflowers, sliced 2cm (¾ inch) thick, including their tender leaves
- 25g (1oz) unsalted butter, melted

For the salad
- 1 white cabbage, cored and finely shredded
- 1 fennel bulb, tough stalks removed, finely sliced
- 15g (½oz) dill
- 15g (½oz) coriander
- 15g (½oz) chives
- 50g (1¾oz) yogurt
- 2 tablespoons extra virgin olive oil
- 1 green chilli (optional)
- juice of 1 lemon, or to taste

To serve (optional)
- cooked grains
- hot sauce (for homemade, see page 75)

IN & OUT OF THE OVEN

TOTAL TIME: **1 HOUR – 1 HOUR 10 MINUTES**

Lentil cottage pie

This is one of those ultimate comfort dishes. It's brilliant when the weather gets a little colder, or equally a great spring dish with a big salad. If you are pushed for time or don't want to make mash, just slice the potatoes thinly, toss in olive oil, then arrange on top of the lentils and bake. I often double the recipe and portion it into individual pie dishes. That way I can batch-make these for the week and, whenever anyone wants one, just pop it in the oven. They also freeze really well, so this makes a great dish to stock the freezer for those weeknights when you don't have a lot of time but want something nutritious. You can stir 200g (7oz) of frozen peas into the lentils when they are done, to add a fresh pop of veg, or serve with green veg or a big crunchy salad. SERVES 4

- 250g (9oz) dried Puy lentils, or green lentils, or 2 × 400g (14oz) cans, drained
- 1kg (2lb 4oz) potatoes, peeled and cut into equal-sized pieces
- 50g (1¾oz) unsalted butter
- 3 tablespoons olive oil
- 1 onion, finely chopped
- 2 celery sticks, finely chopped
- 2 carrots, finely chopped
- 3 garlic cloves, sliced
- 100ml (3½fl oz) white wine, or cider
- 2 × 400g (14oz) cans of plum tomatoes
- 200g (7oz) Cheddar cheese, coarsely grated
- sea salt flakes and black pepper

1. If cooking the lentils from dried, put them in a saucepan with a good pinch of salt and cover well with water. Simmer gently for 20–25 minutes until tender, then drain.

2. Meanwhile, boil the potatoes in a saucepan of well-salted water for about 12–15 minutes until they fall from a knife easily when pierced. Drain thoroughly and mash until smooth with the butter and a good pinch of salt. Set aside.

3. While the potatoes are boiling, heat the oil in a large saucepan over a medium heat and add the onion, celery and carrots. Stir until the vegetables begin to soften; 10–12 minutes.

4. Add the garlic and white wine or cider, let the alcohol evaporate for a minute, then add the canned tomatoes. Either with a wooden spoon or a masher, roughly crush the tomatoes to break them up. Rinse out the tomato cans with half their volume of water and add to the pan. Bubble away for 5 minutes, then add the cooked or canned lentils. Cook together until the sauce has thickened and is clinging to the lentils, seasoning well.

5. Preheat the oven to 200°C/180°C fan (400°F), Gas Mark 6. Spread the lentil mixture evenly in a deep pie dish that will easily accommodate everything, or individual pie dishes. Scatter half the cheese on top, then spoon over dollops of mash for a complete, even covering, trying to form peaks as you go; the idea is that these will crisp up in the oven. Finish with the remaining cheese.

6. Bake the pie in the oven, turning halfway, until bubbling at the edges and golden and crisp on top; it should take 30–40 minutes, or a bit longer if it's been pre-assembled and cooked straight from the fridge. Allow to stand for 15 minutes once it's out of the oven.

TOTAL TIME: **45–55 MINUTES**

Crispy tofu, couscous, pickled onions & tzatziki

This recipe is one of the ways I got my family to eat – actually to request – tofu. You get a really crunchy exterior that you can flavour in any way you want. Try mixing in different spice blends or rubs to suit the flavour profile you are after. This tofu is also great in sandwiches or wraps. If you don't have cucumber, swap in herbs or sliced spring onion. SERVES 4

- 10g (¼oz) ras el hanout
- 50g (1¾oz) cornflour
- 450g (1lb) firm tofu
- 4 tablespoons olive oil
- 300g (10½oz) couscous
- finely grated zest and juice of 2 lemons
- 300ml (½ pint) boiling water
- 200g (7oz) frozen peas, preferably petits pois
- 1 cucumber
- 250g (9oz) yogurt
- 1 teaspoon onion powder (optional)
- 1 teaspoon garlic powder, or 1 garlic clove, grated
- salt and black pepper
- pickled red onions (see page 66, made without sumac), to serve

1. Preheat the oven to 220°C/200°C fan (425°F), Gas Mark 7. Place a baking tray in the oven to heat.

2. In a mixing bowl, mix the ras el hanout with the cornflour and a good pinch of salt. Slice the block of tofu in half across its equator, then each half into 6 slices. Drop them into the cornflour mixture and move around to coat well. Drizzle in 3 tablespoons of the oil and continue to toss the slices in the cornflour; it will start to clump up and these clumps will be the extra-crispy bits. Carry on, pressing and sticking the cornflour to the slices.

3. Remove the hot tray from the oven and arrange the tofu evenly over it. Return to the oven and cook for 20 minutes. Turn the tray 180 degrees, flip the tofu slices and cook for another 20–30 minutes until crisp.

4. Meanwhile, put the remaining 1 tablespoon of oil in a heatproof mixing bowl with the couscous and mix well to coat all the grains. Add all the lemon zest and half the juice with a good pinch of salt, then pour in the measured boiling water. Stir and cover with a plate or lid. In a separate bowl, cover the peas in boiling water. Set both aside for 15 minutes.

5. While the couscous and peas are soaking, grate the cucumber coarsely into a bowl, add a good pinch of salt and mix well. After 15 minutes, squeeze out as much liquid as you can. Mix the cucumber with the yogurt, onion powder if using, and the garlic. Adjust the seasoning to taste.

6. Fluff up the grains of couscous with a fork. Drain the peas and add them to the couscous.

7. Spoon the couscous on to plates alongside the crispy tofu, tzatziki and pickled red onions.

IN & OUT OF THE OVEN

TOTAL TIME: 35–45 MINUTES

Baked polenta with creamed kale

Whack the polenta in the oven – it looks after itself and comes out with the perfect texture – while you crack on with the kale. I love the creamy sauce here, but if you want to swap things up, replace the crème fraîche with a can of plum tomatoes, crushed up and added with the leeks.

Cooking the polenta in this way eliminates the bubbling lava on the stove, but if you want the dish to be ready more quickly, simply cook it in a pan according to the packet instructions and it will be done in just a few minutes. SERVES 4

- 250g (9oz) quick-cook polenta
- 1.25 litres (2 pints) vegetable stock
- 2 tablespoons olive oil
- 3 tablespoons flavourless oil
- 2 onions, sliced from tip to root
- 2 celery sticks, finely sliced
- 2 leeks, cleaned and shredded
- 3 garlic cloves, sliced
- 400g (14oz) cavolo nero or kale, woody stalks discarded, tender stalks finely sliced, leaves torn
- 100ml (3½fl oz) cider, or white wine
- 200g (7oz) crème fraîche
- 15g (½oz) parsley, finely chopped
- salt and black pepper

To serve
- grated hard cheese, such as Spenwood
- chilli oil, or pickled or fermented chillies (for homemade, see page 75)

1. Preheat the oven to 220°C/200°C fan (425°F), Gas Mark 7. In a baking dish, mix the polenta with the stock, olive oil and a good pinch of salt; I use a whisk. Place in the oven and bake for 35–45 minutes, removing from the oven to stir every 10–15 minutes.

2. Meanwhile, heat a saucepan over a medium heat with the flavourless oil and add the onions and celery. Cook for 10 minutes, then add the leeks, garlic and finely sliced tender cavolo nero or kale stalks. Stir well and continue to cook for a further 4 minutes.

3. Add the cavolo nero or kale leaves to the pan with the cider or white wine. Add another pinch of salt. Let the leaves wilt for a minute, then add the crème fraîche. Bring to a bubble and cook for 4–6 minutes until the leaves are tender. Add the parsley with lots of cracked black pepper. Taste and add more seasoning if needed.

4. Serve the polenta straight from the oven with the creamed kale piled on top. Grated cheese and chilli oil, or pickled or fermented chillies, are all welcome.

TOTAL TIME: **35 MINUTES**

Rosemary & Cheddar soda bread scones

I've enjoyed this flavour mix in American biscuits (savoury scones in the UK), and I thought it would work well in soda bread form, especially with nuttier, deeper-flavoured flour. Have a play with different flours and ratios; equally, just use all plain white flour if that's what you have. You can use this as a template to pile in other flavours or ingredients: seeds and nuts are most welcome, lots of herbs, sliced spring onions and spices as well. This mixture also works well when baked as a loaf, when it will need 30 minutes in an oven preheated to 220°C/200°C fan (425°F), Gas Mark 7 and a further 10 minutes at 200°C/180°C fan (400°F), Gas Mark 6, rotating the baking sheet halfway through. These scones are great in the summer with a salad and a boiled egg, or alongside soups or stews in the colder months. MAKES 6

- 250g (9oz) 00 flour (or plain works fine), plus more to dust
- 250g (9oz) malthouse flour, or spelt or wholemeal flour
- 15g (½oz) fine sea salt
- 1 teaspoon bicarbonate of soda
- 250g (9oz) Cheddar cheese, cut into 1cm (½ inch) cubes
- 2 large rosemary sprigs, leaves picked and chopped fairly finely
- 400g (14oz) yogurt

1. Preheat the oven to 220°C/200°C fan (425°F), Gas Mark 7. Line a baking tray with nonstick baking paper.

2. In a mixing bowl, mix the flours with the salt and bicarb, then mix in the cheese and rosemary. Stir in the yogurt to form a rough dough, being careful not to overwork it. Tip the dough out on to a floured work surface and bring it together into a ball. Press the ball lightly to flatten it a little into a circle about 24cm (9½ inches) in diameter and about 4cm (1½ inches) high. With a knife or dough scraper, divide the dough into 6 with decisive cuts.

3. Place the scones on the prepared tray and bake for 15 minutes. Rotate the baking sheet 180 degrees and continue baking for a further 10 minutes.

4. Remove the scones from the oven and allow to cool for as long as you can wait; 5–10 minutes is fine. Eat greedily while still warm and with the cheese oozing.

TOTAL TIME: **1 HOUR 5 MINUTES – 1¼ HOURS**

Seed crackers

I sometimes make this amount in a single baking tray, which results in a more substantial seed bar of sorts, then use those for packed-lunch snacks for my son or myself, rather than for dipping. Try making these your own with your favoured additions, to take the flavour in different directions. Add cumin seeds or cracked black pepper, for instance, or sesame, chia, poppy or nigella seeds work well, too. MAKES 2 TRAYS

- 200g (7oz) linseeds
- 100g (3½oz) chia seeds
- 500ml (18fl oz) boiling water
- 200g (7oz) pumpkin seeds
- 200g (7oz) sunflower seeds
- 50g (1¾oz) cornflour
- 2–3 tablespoons extra virgin olive oil
- 10g (¼oz) sea salt flakes

1. Tip the linseeds and chia seeds into a heatproof mixing bowl and pour in the measured boiling water from the kettle. Leave for 15 minutes while you preheat the oven to 190°C/170°C fan (375°F), Gas Mark 5. Then stir in the rest of the ingredients.

2. Line 2 large (40 × 30cm/16 × 12 inch) baking trays with nonstick baking paper, then spread the mixture as evenly as possible over the trays.

3. Place the baking trays in the oven and bake for 40–50 minutes, rotating the trays on their shelves and with each another halfway, to encourage an even cook. Once the crackers are fragrant and golden, they are done. For the last 5–10 minutes, I carefully flip the crackers on the baking trays to cook the bases further. To do this, carefully grab an end with a clean tea towel and swiftly flip them over.

4. Remove the crackers from the oven and allow them to cool on a wire rack, then break them up and store them in an airtight container. They will keep for around 2 weeks.

COOKING DRIED BEANS.
Yes, on a weeknight

Some kitchen processes take time, but they're worth it, even during the week. Like cooking dried beans. I know people often groan at the idea of cooking beans and other pulses – or even rice or grains – from dried. Yes, it is easier to buy a can, jar or pouch these days and – boom – they are ready to go. And don't get me wrong, I still use cans or jars of beans often; they have saved many a working lunch, or packed lunch, in my house.

But you should try cooking beans and peas from dried, even if you are one of the groaners. Why? Four good reasons. First, because pre-cooked beans don't offer the same variety; there are some brilliant lesser-known (and locally grown) varieties that you don't ever – or at least often – see in pre-cooked form. You can find the bean (or grain) to best express yourself on any given occasion. Second, a can, jar or pouch will not have the same depth of flavour, and more flavourful foods have a direct correlation to those that contain more nutrients (because biology is clever like that). Third, pre-cooked beans are more expensive. And fourth, because – you know what? – I really enjoying soaking and cooking my beans from dried. It is meditative, reassuring, grounding. It puts the power back in your hands.

There is an easy way to fit the process into your day so that it doesn't really require much effort or time, but you end up with a veritable bounty of a base ingredient. Then, over the coming days, you can take that bounty in many different directions depending on your mood, saving time as well as providing you with nutrient-dense food.

Most meals are made better with beans (or flavourful grains, which I'll come to) cooked from scratch, whether it be salads or stews, wraps or sandwiches, as whole beans, crushed or puréed. A few spoonfuls give texture and an added dimension to many dishes. They are a truly versatile, nutritious ingredient that boosts any meal. A creamy bean and crunchy veg salad is my go-to working lunch, with a tangy, vinegar-spiked dressing. No word of a lie, I could happily eat that every day.

Josiah Meldrum of Hodmedod's Wholefoods once told me that the toughness of the skins of beans or pulses isn't to do with salt, as is often claimed; it's to do with acid. So if you want to add flavours like wine or a seasoning of vinegar to your beans or pulses, do so towards the end of the cooking time for the most tender results. It is worth noting, too, that some cooking times can be longer than written on the packet. I tend to double the time, just in case. Or a pressure cooker will cut cooking times to a factor.

So, how to fit dried beans into the working week? I submerge the dried beans in a large bowl of water on the kitchen work surface at breakfast time before heading out for work, then cook them when I'm back in the evening. Or I soak them last thing in the evening before going to bed, then start cooking them over breakfast; that way, they are done before I head out and I know they'll be waiting for dinner when I get back. Either way, soaking beans for about eight hours is good.

I appreciate that cooking them at breakfast time may be a bit of a stretch for some people. Truth be told, I tend to do this when my son has a spell of waking up at 5am, as I have the time then! I guess what I'm trying to highlight is that you can make these processes fit around your timings. Equally, soak beans on Sunday morning and cook them in the evening, when you tend not to be so busy as you are on other nights of the week. After all, Sunday night is technically a weeknight.

There is an argument for soaking grains as well, ideally for at least seven hours, as it makes them more digestible and they cook faster. It also unlocks more nutrients if grains are soaked in acidulated water, adding about 1 tablespoon of lemon juice or vinegar to the soaking liquid for each 200g (7oz) of grains. Grains should be kept in the fridge while soaking, then rinsed really well before cooking. You will need less water, and less time, to cook soaked grains as well, compared to their fully dried versions. Rice, quinoa, oat groats, wheat berries and pearled barley are just some grains that benefit from soaking.

Whether dried beans or grains, give it a go. You won't look back.

WORTH THE WASHING-UP

Here we have an eclectic mix of the meals that get asked for over and over in our house. That's because they're super-tasty dishes that all of us would be happy to eat any day of the year, so I reckon that goes for all of you as well. Most are nevertheless quick to pull together, others can be left to bubble or bake away while you get on with other things (or simply relax) and some can be made ahead and left in the fridge for reheating.

TOTAL TIME: 20–25 MINUTES

Charred leeks, broken eggs, fried capers & dill

This dish is extremely quick to bring together, especially if you are using leftover cooked leeks. As well as a midweek dinner, this can make a great weekend breakfast or lunch dish. Serve it with cooked rice or other grains, or on a good chunky slice of toasted sourdough, to bulk it up to a more substantial offering. SERVES 4

- 4 leeks, cleaned, any really tough green ends trimmed
- flavourless oil, for greasing
- 8 eggs
- 3–4 tablespoons drained capers
- 25g (1oz) dill, chopped
- salt and black pepper

1. Set a large pan of salted water on to boil and fill a large bowl with ice cubes and very cold water. Cut the leeks into even sections. Blanch them for 2–3 minutes until mostly cooked through, then remove with tongs to the ice bath for 3–4 minutes, to stop the cooking. Drain and dry well.

2. Put a griddle pan or heavy-based frying pan over a medium heat. Brush or rub the leeks with oil and add to the pan, weighing them down if you can, to get a maximum contact area. Cook for 2–3 minutes, then flip and repeat on the other side. Watch them, as they colour quickly, and remove once done. They should be collapsing and lightly charred on their exterior.

3. Place a small frying pan – ideally one that has a lid – over a medium heat, add some oil and crack in 4 eggs. Season with a pinch of salt. After they have started to set for a moment, pierce the yolks and run them around the pan to create a marble effect, just enough to spread them around a little. If you have a lid, pop it on to help cook the top more quickly. Leave for 1–2 minutes, then remove to a plate. Repeat to cook the remaining eggs, dividing them between 4 plates, or placing on a platter.

4. Pull the leeks apart slightly and lay them on top of the eggs.

5. Add a small splash of oil to the pan and tip in the capers. Fry these until they start to colour and crisp. Scatter them on top of the leeks, followed by the dill, and finish with a good grind of black pepper.

TOTAL TIME: **20 MINUTES FOR JARRED CHICKPEAS;
1 HOUR – 1 HOUR 10 MINUTES, PLUS SOAKING, FOR DRIED CHICKPEAS**

Orecchiette with chickpeas

I love pasta sauces that come together while the pasta is cooking. This one is lovely and wholesome, great for when the weather starts to warm up a little, and one of those that you can pretty much make year-round. Sub in other green veg, such as shredded cavolo nero, or even sliced courgettes. You can also try adding 100g (3½oz) kalamata olives, pitted and torn into quarters, at the end of cooking, to add another dimension. SERVES 4

- 1 red onion, finely chopped
- 3 tablespoons red wine vinegar
- 350g (12oz) orecchiette
- 4 tablespoons extra virgin olive oil
- 1 onion, finely chopped
- 5 garlic cloves, sliced
- 700g (1lb 9oz) jar of chickpeas, or 2 × 400g (14oz) cans of chickpeas, or 250g (9oz) dried chickpeas, soaked overnight or for 8 hours, cooked and drained, reserving a little of the cooking stock (see pages 166–7 and 200)
- 200g (7oz) baby leaf spinach, or large leaf spinach with the tough stalks removed
- salt

To serve
- chilli flakes, or peperoncino
- 1 lemon, cut into wedges (optional)
- grated hard cheese, such as Spenwood (optional)

1. Mix the red onion and vinegar together with a pinch of salt. Set aside. Get the pasta on to cook in a saucepan of well-salted boiling water.

2. Meanwhile, set a large high-sided frying pan or sauté pan over a medium heat and add the oil and the onion. Cook for 7–10 minutes until it turns translucent.

3. Add the garlic to the pan. Cook for 1 minute until fragrant but not taking on too much colour, then add the chickpeas with their juices, if using a jar, or with a little of their stock if you have cooked your own. Warm through.

4. Once the pasta is al dente, drain, reserving some of the cooking water, and add the pasta to the chickpea pan. Add the spinach and stir in to wilt, loosening the sauce with a splash of the pasta cooking water if needed, as a little brothiness is welcome.

5. Serve in warmed bowls, topped with the chilli flakes or peperoncino and lightly pickled red onion, with lemon wedges and grated cheese alongside, if you like.

WORTH THE WASHING-UP

TOTAL TIME: **45 MINUTES**

Oyster mushroom cheesesteaks with potato salad

Sometimes you just need a super-satisfying meal to blow away any notion of being hungry. This ticks that box and I make these quite often, just as sandwiches. You can swap out the salad for oven chips, if you prefer, but I find the crunchy, mustardy salad is a good foil for the rich cheesey oyster mushrooms. SERVES 4

- 600g (1lb 5oz) new potatoes (I like waxy varieties, but you can use larger potatoes if you prefer), cut into 2cm (¾ inch) cubes
- 8–10 tablespoons mayonnaise
- 4 sub rolls, or Malthouse Muffins (see page 46) work a treat
- 500g (1lb 2oz) oyster mushrooms
- flavourless oil, for drizzling and cooking
- 30g (1oz) cornflour
- 3 celery sticks, finely sliced
- 3–4 tablespoons drained capers
- 1–2 tablespoons Dijon mustard
- 2 onions, chunkily sliced
- 2 peppers (green are good but a mix also works), cored, deseeded and chunkily sliced
- 150g (5½oz) smoked Cheddar cheese, or goats' Cheddar cheese, or your favourite cheese, sliced
- 15g (½oz) chives, finely sliced
- salt and black pepper

1. Add the potatoes to a pan of well-salted boiling water and cook for 5–7 minutes until just cooked through. Once just tender, drain and set aside.

2. Spread half the mayonnaise over the cut sides of your rolls or muffins and toast them cut side down in a large frying pan until evenly golden and crisp. Set aside.

3. Put the oyster mushrooms in a large mixing bowl, drizzle with 2–3 tablespoons of oil and use your hands to spread the oil around to coat them well, trying not to break them up. Then sprinkle in the cornflour and a good pinch or so of salt. Toss well to get as much stuck on as possible.

4. Heat 1 tablespoon of oil in the pan. Add the mushrooms and cook until crisp and golden; 3–5 minutes each side. Remove and set aside.

5. While the mushrooms are cooking, combine the potatoes with the rest of the mayonnaise, the celery, capers and mustard. Mix well with a pinch of salt and a good cracking of black pepper. Taste and add any element you think needs a boost.

6. Preheat the grill. Add another 2 tablespoons of oil to the pan and tip in the onions with a good pinch of salt. Fry, stirring occasionally, for 3–4 minutes, then add the peppers. Cook for 3–4 minutes more until wilted but still with texture.

7. Divide the mixture from the pan evenly between the rolls or muffins. Top with the mushrooms, then the cheese. Place the cheesesteaks under the hot grill until the cheese is melted, then serve with the potato salad scattered with the chives.

WORTH THE WASHING-UP

TOTAL TIME: 30-40 MINUTES FOR CANNED CHICKPEAS;
1 HOUR 10 MINUTES - 1 HOUR 20 MINUTES, PLUS SOAKING, FOR DRIED CHICKPEAS

Chickpea curry with spinach theplas

This curry has become somewhat of a staple in my house, as it is simple to make, rich from the sauce but with pops of freshness from the peppers. Pair it with these quick and simple *theplas*, which are a staple of Gujurati cuisine. The *theplas* also work well on their own, as a packed lunch option, and can be reheated in a pan for breakfast with fried eggs. The curry can be made independently of the *theplas*, and also goes very well with rice. SERVES 4

1. Place a saucepan over a medium heat with a small amount of oil and add the spinach for the theplas. Stir until wilted, then remove and allow to cool.

2. Now start the curry. Add a couple more tablespoons of oil to the pan with the onions and cook for 8–10 minutes, adding the peppers halfway through. Add the spices and cook for 30 seconds, then add the garlic with the tomatoes, crushing them with a wooden spoon or a masher. Add the canned chickpeas with their liquid or your home-cooked chickpeas with a little of their stock and the coconut milk, then bring to a simmer and bubble away gently for 10–15 minutes to reduce the liquid and concentrate the flavours. If it gets too dry, add a splash of water.

3. Meanwhile, return to the theplas. Mix the flours together in a mixing bowl. In another bowl, mix the yogurt, ginger, garlic and spices. Chop the spinach and add to the flours, then stir in the yogurt mixture to form a dough. Tip out on to a work surface and gently knead to bring together, then divide into 4. Roll each piece out to a circle 26–30cm (10½–12 inches) in diameter, or whatever diameter will fit in your largest frying pan. Cook, one at a time, in a dry frying pan over a medium–low heat for 3–4 minutes on each side.

4. Serve the theplas, cut into triangles, with the curry, scattered with the coriander.

For the *theplas*
- flavourless oil, for cooking
- 200g (7oz) baby spinach
- 200g (7oz) wholemeal flour
- 100g (3½oz) gram (chickpea) flour
- 200g (7oz) yogurt
- ½ thumb of fresh root ginger, peeled and finely grated
- 2 garlic cloves, finely grated
- 1 teaspoon ground turmeric
- ½ teaspoon ground coriander
- ½ teaspoon ground cumin

For the curry
- 2 onions, chopped
- 2 peppers (any colour), cored, deseeded and chopped
- 1 tablespoon curry powder
- 1 teaspoon ground cumin
- 1 teaspoon Kashmiri chilli powder
- 3 garlic cloves, sliced
- 400g (14oz) can of plum tomatoes
- 2 × 400g (14oz) cans of chickpeas, or 250g (9oz) dried chickpeas, soaked overnight or for 8 hours, cooked and drained, reserving a little of the cooking stock (see pages 166–7 and 200)
- 400g (14oz) can of coconut milk
- 15g (½oz) coriander leaves

WORTH THE WASHING-UP

TOTAL TIME: **30–40 MINUTES, PLUS CHILLING**

Cheddar semolina, for summer

What's better than ripe tomatoes and herbs as a support to soft-but-crispy semolina? You can shape the semolina however you please, or to whatever shape best fits your pan. I particularly like serving this to those of an age to remember having semolina as a dessert at school; it is rather fun to see their reactions… SERVES 4

- flavourless oil, for greasing and cooking
- 500ml (18fl oz) vegetable stock
- 500ml (18fl oz) whole milk
- 250g (9oz) semolina
- 200g (7oz) hard cheese (Cheddar is good, but try other similar cheese), grated
- 800g (1lb 12oz) ripe tomatoes
- 3–5 tablespoons olive oil, to taste
- 2–3 tablespoons white wine vinegar, or other vinegar, or even lemon juice, to taste
- 3 spring onions, finely sliced
- 25g (1oz) dill, finely chopped, or other soft herbs, such as basil or parsley
- salt and black pepper

1. Oil a 30 × 24cm (12 × 9½ inch) baking tray, line it with nonstick baking paper and oil the paper, too. Bring the stock and milk to a simmer, add a good couple of pinches of salt, then rain in the semolina, whisking as you go. Cook for 3–4 minutes until thickened, then stir through the cheese. Check the seasoning and add more if needed.

2. Pour the semolina into the prepared baking tray and spread out as evenly as possible, but some bumps are okay. Place in the freezer if you have space, fridge if not, or use smaller trays! Leave for 20–30 minutes until bouncy and set.

3. Meanwhile, slice your tomatoes and fan them out either on plates or a serving platter, or cut them into chunks and put them into a bowl. Dress them with the oil and vinegar to taste and add salt and pepper. Mix in the spring onions and herbs, or just scatter them on top.

4. Heat a heavy-based frying pan or flat griddle over a medium heat. Tip out the set semolina on to a work surface, then cut into triangles or squares. Add some oil to the pan, followed by as many pieces of semolina as will fit comfortably; don't over-crowd them. Fry until golden, then flip and do the same on the other side; 2–3 minutes each side should be enough. Serve with the tomato salad.

TOTAL TIME: 1¼ HOURS FOR HOMEMADE PASTA; 35 MINUTES FOR SHOP-BOUGHT

Squash pasta with toasted hazelnuts & crispy sage

I appreciate that making pasta may not fit with a weeknight meal agenda, but I put the recipe here in case you want it as part of your wind-down routine! Otherwise, of course, use 500g (1lb 2oz) dried pasta. This is a go-to of mine, as the sauce is essentially made while the pasta is boiling… well, that is, if you are using dried pasta and don't count toasting the hazelnuts! But you get my drift…

SERVES 4

- 400g (14oz) 00 flour, plus more to dust
- 4 eggs
- 50g (1¾oz) blanched hazelnuts
- olive oil, for cooking
- 25g (1oz) sage, leaves picked
- 1 onion, finely chopped
- 500g (1lb 2oz) prepared Crown Prince squash, butternut squash or pumpkin, chopped roughly into 1cm (½ inch) pieces
- 250ml (9fl oz) water
- 150g (5½oz) goats' cheese, or Roquefort, or hard cheese such as Spenwood, finely grated or chopped, plus more (optional)

To serve
- salt
- extra virgin olive oil, to serve (optional)

1. Put the flour and eggs in a stand mixer bowl fitted with a dough hook and knead to form a smooth dough. Leave this to rest on a work surface under the upturned mixing bowl.

2. Preheat the oven to 200°C/180°C fan (400°F), Gas Mark 6. Roast the hazelnuts on a small tray for 10–12 minutes until golden. Set aside. When cool enough, crush them slightly, or chop through them.

3. Meanwhile, heat 3 tablespoons of oil in a large high-sided frying pan over a medium–low heat. Add the sage leaves and cook, gently moving around, until they are crisp and stop bubbling, but be careful not to let them burn. Remove to a plate lined with kitchen paper. Add the onion to the pan with a good pinch of salt and cook until it is translucent; 10–12 minutes. Follow with the squash or pumpkin and pour in the measured water. Cook over a medium heat for 8–10 minutes until the squash or pumpkin is cooked through, adding a splash more water if needed.

4. Roll out the pasta to 1mm thick, either using a machine or a rolling pin, dusting with extra flour to stop it sticking. Cut into strips, dust with a little flour and keep on a small baking tray until ready to cook.

5. Crush the squash or pumpkin mixture a little with a masher in the pan. Bring a saucepan of well-salted water to the boil and cook the pasta until just done. Drain well, reserving the cooking water, and add to the squash or pumpkin with the cheese and a ladle of the pasta cooking water. Toss to coat the pasta with the sauce until the cheese is beginning to melt, loosening with more cooking water if needed. Serve with the sage leaves and hazelnuts on top. A drizzle of extra virgin olive oil – as well as more cheese – is always welcome.

WORTH THE WASHING-UP

TOTAL TIME: **50 MINUTES – 1 HOUR FOR DRIED LENTILS; 45 MINUTES FOR CANNED LENTILS**

Austrian-style lentils with giant bread dumplings

I was served this dish in a bistro while on a job in Austria during a drizzly November and it was just the ticket. The lentils are traditionally flavoured with a baharat spice blend and served with one giant bread dumpling for each person. I've replicated the spice blend here, but for speed you could seek out a shop-bought version. For ease of making, and speed of cooking, I have broken the iceberg of a dumpling into three here. SERVES 4

- 2 tablespoons flavourless oil
- 3 onions, finely chopped
- 1 carrot, finely chopped or grated
- 2–3 tablespoons sweet paprika
- 1 teaspoon ground cumin
- 1 teaspoon ground coriander
- ¼ teaspoon ground cinnamon
- a few gratings of nutmeg
- 1 star anise
- 250g (9oz) dried green lentils (Puy or others that hold their shape work well), or 2 × 400g (14oz) cans, drained
- 1 litre (1¾ pints) vegetable stock, or 300ml (½ pint) if you are using pre-cooked lentils
- 200ml (7fl oz) white wine
- salt
- 15g (½oz) parsley, finely chopped, to serve

For the dumplings
- 2 eggs, lightly beaten
- 250ml (9fl oz) whole milk
- 50g (1¾oz) plain flour
- 1 tablespoon baking powder
- 400g (14oz) stale crustless bread, cut into small cubes

1. To make the dumplings, beat the eggs with the milk in a bowl. In a separate bowl, mix the flour and baking powder with the bread cubes. Then pour in the milk mixture and scrunch it together with your hands until well combined. The mixture may appear too wet when you first make it, but after a few minutes it will come together as the bread absorbs the liquid. Set aside.

2. Put the oil in a saucepan over a medium heat. Add the onions with a good pinch of salt and cook for 8–10 minutes until softened. Remove half the onions and mix them into the dumpling mixture. Add the carrot to the pan with the remaining onions and cook for a further 4–6 minutes. Add the spices to the pan and cook for another minute, stirring, then tip in the lentils, stock and wine. Bring to a simmer and cook the dried lentils for 25–35 minutes until just tender, or cooked lentils for 10–15 minutes just until all the flavours are happy together.

3. Meanwhile, set a very wide pan of salted water over a high heat to come to a simmer. Shape the dumpling dough into 12 equal balls, wetting your hands before forming each to keep them from sticking. Add them to the simmering water, one at a time, and cook for 10–12 minutes.

4. Spoon out the lentils and serve with the dumplings on top, scattered with the parsley.

TOTAL TIME: 1¼–1½ HOURS, PLUS RESTING AND STANDING

Feta tart with tomato & olive salad

A one-foot-in-the-cupboard type of recipe, as feta is a staple in my fridge and remains stable for ages, while the other ingredients you tend to have in. If you don't have a blender, the feta can be grated or crumbled; you just won't achieve the same smooth texture.

If you are using ready-made pastry rather than making it from scratch, this recipe is super quick to bring together. It is great to whip up if you have people coming over, as it wows and you can adjust the toppings to your taste, or to what is available and in season. Spreading a layer of reduced tomato sauce, or black olive tapenade, over the pastry before topping with the feta mix works brilliantly, too. Swapping the tomatoes for blanched, chilled and sliced asparagus is lovely in springtime.

SERVES 8

For the pastry
- 325g (11½oz) sheet of ready-made puff pastry

Or, for homemade
- 250g (9oz) wholemeal flour, or white if you want, plus more to dust
- 125g (4½oz) unsalted butter, well chilled and chopped into cubes
- 1 teaspoon fine sea salt
- 2–3 tablespoons very cold water

For the filling
- 200g (7oz) feta cheese
- 4 eggs
- 150ml (¼ pint) double cream
- 100ml (3½fl oz) whole milk

For the topping
- 250g (9oz) cherry tomatoes, halved across the equator
- 100g (3½oz) kalamata olives, pitted and torn into chunks
- 1 small red onion, finely sliced
- 3 tablespoons red wine vinegar
- 25g (1oz) basil, leaves picked
- 2–3 tablespoons extra virgin olive oil

1. If making the pastry, in a large mixing bowl, combine the flour, butter and salt. Roughly rub in the butter, massaging the flour into it. Scrappy is better here; it doesn't want to be too evenly incorporated, as larger chunks help simulate rough puff pastry. Stir in 1–2 tablespoons of the measured water. If that feels enough to bring it together, then carry on, otherwise add a little more. Bring the dough together, then turn out on to a work surface and bring together fully. Cover with the upturned mixing bowl and let sit for 15 minutes.

2. Dust the work surface with flour, place the dough in the middle, sprinkle with some more flour and roll it out in long strokes, going one direction at a time and avoiding rolling back and forth over the pastry, until the diameter of the circle is 30cm (12 inches). Roll the pastry on to the rolling pin. Lift it up and over a 23cm (9 inch) round deep tart tin, then unroll the pastry over the tin. Or unroll your bought pastry over the tin, rolling it out a little more to fit first, if necessary. Lift the edges and let the pastry fall into the tin, gently coaxing it into the edges and trying not to stretch the dough. Any extra pastry that comes over the edge, just tuck over. Place in the fridge to rest for 30–45 minutes.

3. Preheat the oven to 220°C/200°C fan (425°F), Gas Mark 7.

4. Dot around the pastry with a fork, cover with nonstick baking paper and fill with dry rice or baking beans. Bake in the oven for 15 minutes. Remove the paper and rice or beans and bake for a further 10 minutes. Remove from the oven and set aside.

5. Reduce the oven temperature to 180°C/160°C fan (350°F), Gas Mark 4.

6. Put the filling ingredients into a blender and mix on low to fully incorporate everything and completely break down the feta. If you don't have a blender, just crumble the feta as finely as you can. Pour into the tart case. Bake for 35–45 minutes until the edges appear set but the middle is still wobbly. Ideally, check the centre temperature with a probe thermometer: once it measures 72°C (162°F), it is done.

7. Remove the tart from the oven and allow to cool and finish cooking: 15 minutes is fine; 30 minutes is great. Equally, serving at room temperature is fine, so the tart can be made ahead and be ready to go once guests arrive. Combine the topping ingredients in a bowl and spoon over each slice.

TOTAL TIME: 50 MINUTES – 1 HOUR 5 MINUTES

Red lentil, aubergine & potato bake

This takes inspiration from moussaka but is its own thing. You do have the layers, with the red lentils as a base, topped with grilled aubergine and a creamy sauce, but the potatoes are on top, so they get some crispy edges. This is satisfying and comforting as is, or a salad or some simple blanched green veg goes splendidly alongside.

SERVES 4

- olive oil, for cooking
- 2 onions, roughly chopped
- 3 garlic cloves, sliced
- 1 tablespoon dried oregano
- pinch of ground cinnamon
- 250g (9oz) red lentils
- 1 litre (1¾ pints) vegetable stock
- 600g (1lb 5oz) potatoes, scrubbed and cut into 1cm (½ inch) slices
- 2 aubergines, total weight about 700g (1lb 9oz), sliced into 2cm (¾ inch) rounds
- 250g (9oz) ricotta cheese
- 125g (4½oz) yogurt
- ½ nutmeg
- 15g (½oz) parsley, finely chopped
- salt

1. Pick a saucepan that will fit the lentils, as they will double in size once they absorb the liquid. Over a medium heat, add 3 tablespoons of oil. Tip in the onions and cook for 6–8 minutes until beginning to soften. Add the garlic, oregano and cinnamon, cook for a minute, then follow with the lentils and the stock. Bring to a simmer and cook for 15–20 minutes until just tender. The lentils want to retain a little bite at this stage, as they will carry on cooking in the baking dish.

2. Meanwhile, bring a pan of salted water to the boil. Add the potatoes and blanch until just tender. Remove and spread out on a tray to cool.

3. Heat a griddle pan or a large frying pan over a medium-high heat. Rub the aubergine slices with oil and sprinkle with salt. Cook for 2–3 minutes on each side until golden and just soft.

4. Preheat the oven to 200°C/180°C fan (400°F), Gas Mark 6. Whisk the ricotta and yogurt together with a good pinch of salt and grate in the ½ nutmeg.

5. Tip the lentils into an ovenproof dish; mine is 30 × 20cm (12 × 8 inches). Add the aubergine slices in an even layer. Top with the ricotta sauce, then the potato slices in a neat layer. Bake in the oven for 25–35 minutes.

WORTH THE WASHING-UP

TOTAL TIME: 35–40 MINUTES

Goats' cheese polenta with spiced aubergines & dates

Sticky spiced aubergines on a bed of pillowy, creamy polenta. Sounds good, eats just as good, as well as being pretty no-nonsense and easy to pull together. I have made this with cream cheese in place of the soft goats' cheese and it is equally tasty. The aubergine mix also works brilliantly on a big chunk of toast with some ricotta salata or hard goats' cheese grated over. SERVES 4

- 750g (1lb 10oz) aubergines (about 3), cut into 2–3cm (¾–1¼ inch) cubes
- olive oil, for cooking
- 1 red onion, or 2 banana shallots, finely chopped
- 1 celery stick, finely chopped
- 3 garlic cloves, sliced
- 2 tablespoons ras el hanout
- 125g (4½oz) dates, pitted and finely chopped
- 500ml (18fl oz) whole milk
- 250ml (9fl oz) water
- 150g (5½oz) quick-cook polenta
- 150g (5½oz) soft goats' cheese, roughly sliced or cubed
- 15g (½oz) parsley, finely chopped
- 10g (¼oz) mint, leaves picked
- salt

1. Preheat the oven to 220°C/200°C fan (425°F), Gas Mark 7. Toss the cubed aubergines in oil with a sprinkle of salt and spread them evenly over 1 or 2 baking trays. Roast for 20 minutes, then shake the trays and rotate them. Continue cooking until golden and cooked through; a further 10–15 minutes should get you there.

2. Meanwhile, heat 2 tablespoons of oil in a frying pan that will eventually fit the cooked aubergines. Add the onion or shallots and celery with a pinch of salt and cook gently over a medium–low heat for 10 minutes. Add the garlic and cook for a further 2–3 minutes. Follow with the ras el hanout and dates, toast the spice for a minute, then turn off the heat.

3. In a separate saucepan, bring the milk and measured water to just below a simmer. Stream in the polenta while whisking. Keep cooking over a medium heat until the mixture starts to thicken. Keep going until you have a molten lava consistency, which will be after about 2 minutes. Add the cheese with a pinch of salt and stir to melt and fully incorporate it.

4. Once the aubergines are done, toss in the frying pan and mix well with the date and onion or shallot mixture. Add the parsley and mix to combine. Spoon the polenta on to plates, top with the aubergine mix and scatter with the mint leaves to finish.

WORTH THE WASHING-UP

TOTAL TIME: **50 MINUTES – 1 HOUR, PLUS COOLING**

Sweet potato scarpaccia

Slicing the potatoes and the onions is the majority of the work for this recipe. Mixing them with batter and getting them in the oven so that you can get on with whatever else you like is the idea. This is great as a light meal with a big salad, and it reheats a treat, so works well being made ahead and kept in the fridge. Throwing some finely sliced jalapeños into the mix works very well, if you fancy it. SERVES 4

- 100g (3½oz) polenta
- 50g (1¾oz) cornflour
- 2 rosemary sprigs, leaves picked and finely chopped
- 4 eggs, lightly beaten
- 100ml (3½fl oz) water
- 50–75ml (2–2½fl oz) olive oil
- 700g (1lb 9oz) sweet potatoes, scrubbed and thinly sliced, 5mm (¼ inch) or thinner
- 2 red onions, sliced
- 100–150g (3½–5½oz) hard cheese, such as Spenwood (other hard sheep's or cows' cheeses work fine too), finely grated
- salt and black pepper

1. Preheat the oven to 220°C/200°C fan (425°F), Gas Mark 7. Line a 40 × 30cm (16 × 12 inch) baking tray with nonstick baking paper.

2. Tip the polenta, cornflour and rosemary into a large mixing bowl and stir to combine. In another bowl, mix the eggs with the measured water and 50ml (2fl oz) of the olive oil. Season well with salt and black pepper. Mix this into the dry ingredients, then add the sweet potatoes and red onions along with 100g (3½oz) of the cheese. Toss to coat the vegetables well.

3. Brush half the remaining olive oil over the baking tray and spread the mixture out evenly. Drizzle over the final part of the oil. If you want the extra cheese, scatter it over the top.

4. Bake for 25 minutes, then rotate the tray by 180 degrees and continue to bake until cooked through and golden at the edges and on top; 10–20 minutes more.

5. Remove to a wire rack for 15 minutes, then cut into 4 pieces and serve.

TOTAL TIME: **25 MINUTES**

Asparagus & spinach pasta with black olive breadcrumbs

You can make your own pasta here (see page 181), if you have the time. Otherwise, use your favourite dried pasta – rigatoni work well but I also switch allegiance between tagliatelle and square-cut spaghetti – and the asparagus and breadcrumbs will come together in the time the pasta takes to cook. This also works well without the pasta as a side or with your choice of grain, such as rice or pearled spelt.

When it's in season, swap the spinach for wild garlic leaves as a lovely alternative. SERVES 4

- 500g (1lb 2oz) dried pasta
- 400g (14oz) baby spinach (or see recipe introduction)
- 50g (1¾oz) butter
- 30g (1oz) hard cheese, such as Spenwood, grated (optional)
- finely grated zest and juice of 1–2 lemons, to taste
- 300g (10½oz) sourdough bread, blitzed to crumbs
- 2 tablespoons extra virgin olive oil
- 100g (3½oz) kalamata olives, or other deep-flavoured black olives, pitted and torn in half
- 2–3 tablespoons drained capers
- 10g (¼oz) chives, finely sliced
- 20 asparagus spears, tough woody bases snapped off
- salt and black pepper

1. Bring a large pan of well-salted water to the boil. Add the pasta to the water and cook it according to the packet instructions.

2. Meanwhile, bring a second decent-sized pan of well-salted water to the boil. Once up to a bubble, add the spinach and push down to blanch it. After 30 seconds, remove it with a slotted spoon to a blender, or use a mixing bowl and a stick blender, leaving the water in the pan. Don't worry about bringing across excess liquid to the blender, as it will help the spinach to blend better. Add the butter, and the cheese if you want, and blend until smooth, then taste and season with salt and black pepper, adding lemon juice to taste.

3. In a small frying pan, toast the breadcrumbs in the extra virgin olive oil until golden and crisp, then stir in the olives, capers, chives and lemon zest.

4. Add the asparagus and a good pinch of salt to the spinach cooking water and blanch for 3–4 minutes until tender, then drain. Toss the cooked pasta in the spinach, then divide between plates – or serve on a platter – top with the asparagus, scatter over the olive breadcrumbs and serve.

TOTAL TIME: 35–45 MINUTES

Squash saag

This won't win any authenticity prizes, but I love it for scratching the curry itch while being fresh and packed with flavour: vegetal from the spinach, with pops of sweet squash. As you might expect, it is great with rice and/or naan or other Indian breads, but I do like it with the Potato-stuffed Flatbreads (see page 54). If you find fresh and fragrant curry leaves, freeze them and use straight from the freezer. SERVES 4

- 600g (1lb 5oz) prepared squash or pumpkin, cut into rough 2cm (¾ inch) cubes
- flavourless oil, for cooking
- 600g (1lb 5oz) baby spinach
- 1 onion, roughly chopped
- 4 garlic cloves, sliced
- 1 small thumb of fresh root ginger, peeled and sliced
- 2 green chillies, sliced
- 1 teaspoon ground cumin
- 1 teaspoon ground coriander
- ½ teaspoon ground turmeric
- 4–6 dried chillies
- 2 tablespoons coconut flakes
- handful of fresh curry leaves (optional)
- 1 tablespoon brown mustard seeds
- salt

1. Preheat the oven to 220°C/200°C fan (425°F), Gas Mark 7. Toss the squash or pumpkin in 1–2 tablespoons of oil with a good pinch of salt. Lay evenly on a baking tray and bake until golden and soft when pierced with a knife; 25–35 minutes.

2. Meanwhile, in a pan of well-salted boiling water, blanch the spinach for 15 seconds, then remove to a bowl of iced water to cool. You don't have to chill the spinach, but it does help to preserve the bright colour. Keep some of the spinach cooking water in case you need it to loosen the curry.

3. In a saucepan over a medium–low heat, add 2 tablespoons of oil and the onion and cook until soft and translucent; 8–10 minutes should do. Add the garlic, ginger and green chillies and cook for a further 3 minutes, then add the cumin, coriander and turmeric. Stir in and cook for a further minute.

4. Take off the heat and tip into a blender with the drained spinach. Blitz, loosening with the reserved spinach cooking water to help get things moving. Taste and add more salt if needed.

5. Heat 1–2 tablespoons of oil in a small pan. When hot, add the dried chillies, coconut, curry leaves, if using, and mustard seeds. Cook, while stirring, for 1–2 minutes until fragrant. Take off the heat.

6. Serve the roast squash or pumpkin with the spinach sauce, topped with the dried chilli and coconut mix.

WORTH THE WASHING-UP

TOTAL TIME: **40–45 MINUTES**

Mushroom hotpot with herb dumplings

I love a suet dumpling as it reminds me of my childhood years and the texture just can't really be beaten, plus they are so simple to assemble and take moments to cook. The Suma brand sells a good-quality veg suet, so it's worth trying to find that. Canned lentils are the fast-track to success here but if you're cooking lentils from scratch, use 100g (3½oz) dried lentils and follow the instructions on page 156. SERVES 4

- 6 tablespoons olive oil
- 1kg (2lb 4oz) mixed mushrooms (chestnut, oyster, button, portobello), roughly sliced or torn, depending on size and type
- 1 onion, roughly chopped
- 2 carrots, chopped
- 1 leek, cleaned and thickly sliced
- 3 garlic cloves, sliced
- 250g (9oz) cooked or canned lentils (drained weight), ideally Puy, but others work fine (see recipe introduction)
- 100ml (3½fl oz) white wine, or cider
- 1 litre (1¾ pints) hot vegetable stock
- salt and black pepper

For the dumplings
- 300g (10½oz) plain flour
- 2 tablespoons baking powder
- 15g (½oz) thyme, leaves picked and roughly chopped
- 150g (5½oz) vegetable suet, or unsalted butter cut into small cubes
- 10–15 tablespoons cold water

1. In a large pan with a lid that will fit everything eventually, heat half the oil over a medium–high heat. Add the mushrooms and cook for 4–6 minutes until softened and taking on some colour. Remove to a bowl or plate, being sure to keep any juices that come out.

2. Reduce the heat to medium and tip in the onion and carrots. Cook for 10 minutes, then add the leek and garlic. Cook for a further 5 minutes until everything is soft, then return the mushrooms and add the lentils, followed by the wine or cider. Bring to a bubble for a minute, then pour in the hot stock. Taste for seasoning and adjust to taste.

3. While the stock is coming up to a simmer, mix the flour with the baking powder in a bowl, adding the thyme and suet or butter. Bring the mix together with enough of the measured water to make a dough. You can always add more water, so go steadily. Shape 16 walnut-sized pieces from the dough.

4. Place the dumplings into the broth. When they are all in, place a lid on the pan, reduce the heat to low and allow the dumplings to cook for 10–12 minutes. They will look fluffy and risen when done, but if you are unsure whether they are ready, pull one out, cut it in half and check it is fluffy throughout. Serve immediately.

TOTAL TIME: 15–20 MINUTES

Basil pasta with peas & crunchy crumbs

A sort of green mac-and-cheese type of affair, which wasn't the plan as I'm not a massive mac-and-cheese fan, but there is something about the freshness of basil that lifts this. Try stirring 1 tablespoon of Dijon mustard into the finished pasta for an extra dimension, or some chilli flakes wouldn't go amiss. I favour pasta shells for this, but any shape coated in silky basil bechamel with little pops of freshness from the peas is a win in my book. The basil sauce can be made ahead and kept, covered, in the fridge. It's also brilliant in lasagne, or mix it with grated cheese, spread on toast and grill, like a rarebit.

You can make this more of a dinner-party recipe by topping with fried chanterelles. SERVES 4

- 50g (1¾oz) basil
- 50g (1¾oz) unsalted butter
- 50g (1¾oz) flour
- 500ml (18fl oz) whole milk
- 400g (14oz) pasta shells (I use spelt pasta)
- 200g (7oz) frozen peas, preferably petits pois
- 100g (3½oz) breadcrumbs
- 1–2 tablespoons extra virgin olive oil
- 100g (3½oz) hard cheese, such as Spenwood, finely grated
- salt and black pepper

1. Bring a saucepan of water to the boil and fill a bowl with ice cubes and a little water. First blanch the basil in the boiling water for 15 seconds, then retrieve it with a slotted spoon and immediately add to the ice bath to cool completely. Drain and gently squeeze out obvious excess water, but it doesn't have to be ultra-crushed.

2. Melt the butter with the flour in a saucepan over a medium–low heat. Allow this to cook out well, toasting the flour. When the mixture smells nutty and looks golden, start adding the milk and whisking continuously until it has all been incorporated (I do this in 2 batches). Bring gently to a bubble and allow the mixture to thicken, while stirring with the whisk. Take off the heat, add the basil and blitz it in with a stick blender. Season well with salt and pepper, then cover and set aside.

3. Meanwhile, bring a pan of well-salted water to the boil and add your pasta. Cook until just before you like it, tipping in the peas for the last 30 seconds.

4. Toast the breadcrumbs in a small frying pan with 1–2 tablespoons oil and a pinch of salt until golden and crisp.

5. Drain the pasta, reserving a cup of the cooking water, and return the pasta to the pan. Stir the basil sauce into the pasta with half the cheese, loosening it with some of the pasta cooking water if needed: you're aiming for something that relaxes on the plate and isn't stiff.

6. Serve the pasta with the remaining cheese and breadcrumbs to scatter over the top.

WORTH THE WASHING-UP

TOTAL TIME: **50 MINUTES – 1 HOUR, PLUS SOAKING, FOR DRIED PEAS; 25–30 MINUTES FOR CANNED/JARRED PEAS**

Refried carlin peas

I like my refried beans a bit wetter than you often see them, so in a way, this is reminiscent of a chilli, and I do often serve it on cooked grains. It's a great nutritional platform to top with whatever you have, so it's good for clearing out the veg drawer. Add any bits of veg that you have – finely chopped carrot, cabbage, potato – and it will all add to the flavour. If I'm rushing out the door in the morning but want something proper for dinner, I will throw some beans in a bowl to soak while I'm out. That way, the waiting time is done and you can just get cooking when you're home. If you haven't got carlin peas, try the recipe with different pea or chickpea varieties instead. SERVES 4

1. If cooking soaked dried peas or beans, drain and rinse them. Put them in a saucepan with plenty of water and bring to the boil. Cover and simmer for 40–50 minutes until they are tender. Meanwhile, in another pan over a medium heat, add the oil, onions and a good pinch of salt. Cook for 10–15 minutes until the onions are soft and translucent.

2. Add the garlic, spices and oregano to the onions, stir, and then follow with your drained cooked peas or beans, along with a couple of ladles of their stock, or the liquid from the cans or jar if using ready-cooked. Bring to a simmer and let it bubble for 10 minutes.

3. Mix together the onion or shallots, coriander stalks and citrus juice with a pinch of salt. Set aside.

4. Check the seasoning of the peas or beans, adding the vinegar to taste, then either serve straight away or leave off the heat to let the flavours marry further, as they will improve with time (and this is great after a couple of days in the fridge). Serve on a bed of grains with the onion or shallot topping and scattered with the coriander leaves, with the fermented chillies or hot sauce, if you like.

- 250g (9oz) dried carlin peas, or black chickpeas, or other suitable dried beans of your choice, soaked overnight or for 8 hours (see pages 166–7), or 2 × 400g (14oz) cans of beans, or 1 large (700g/1lb 9oz) jar
- 3 tablespoons olive oil
- 2 red onions, or brown onions, finely chopped
- 3 garlic cloves, sliced, or 1 good heaped teaspoon garlic powder
- 1 heaped teaspoon ground coriander
- 1 heaped teaspoon paprika, sweet, or hot, or a blend
- 1 teaspoon dried oregano
- 1 teaspoon or so of wine vinegar, or cider vinegar, to taste
- sea salt flakes

For the topping
- 1 onion, or 2 banana shallots, finely chopped
- 10g (¼oz) coriander, leaves picked, stalks finely chopped
- juice of 1 lemon or lime, or a splash of cider vinegar

To serve
- cooked grains of choice
- fermented chillies or hot sauce (for homemade, see page 75), (optional but good)

TOTAL TIME: **20–25 MINUTES**

Creamy mushroom tofu broth with noodles

A really quick and delicious meal to bring together. The broth can be used as a sauce for leafy green vegetables, too, such as Brussels sprouts and chestnuts, steamed Savoy cabbage wedges or leeks; in this case, don't add as much water to rehydrate the mushrooms initially. You could also add battered and fried tofu or aubergine chunks on top, to bulk it out a bit. It's a lovely creamy, savoury base sauce that you can take in many directions. Use pearled spelt, rice or buckwheat instead of the noodles, if you prefer; just go with your favourite.

SERVES 4

- 2 onions, roughly chopped
- 15g (½oz) fresh root ginger, washed and finely sliced
- 3 tablespoons flavourless oil (sunflower or groundnut are good)
- 2 garlic cloves, sliced
- 300g (10½oz) silken tofu
- 10g (¼oz) white miso paste
- 30g (1oz) dried shiitake mushrooms, soaked in 500ml (18fl oz) just-boiled water
- 2–3 tablespoons soy sauce, to taste
- 2–3 tablespoons brown rice vinegar, to taste
- 400g (14oz) noodles

To serve (all optional)
- finely sliced spring onions
- blanched green beans
- sheets of nori
- togarashi seasoning
- black sesame seeds
- sliced red chilli
- coriander leaves

1. In a small saucepan, cook the onions with the ginger in the oil until the onions are soft and translucent; it will take 12–15 minutes. When you are 5 minutes in, add the garlic.

2. Tip the contents of the pan into a blender and add the tofu, miso, half the mushrooms and all the mushroom stock that has formed in the mushroom-soaking bowl, adding 2 tablespoons each of the soy and rice vinegar. Blend until smooth. Taste and add more soy or vinegar as needed. Return to the pan and warm through. If the mixture needs to be looser, add water until you like the consistency.

3. Slice the remaining mushrooms.

4. Meanwhile, cook the noodles according to the packet instructions, then drain and divide between warmed bowls with the broth. Top with the sliced mushrooms, spring onions and any other toppings you are using.

WORTH THE WASHING-UP

BATCH-COOKING: the über-hack

Maybe it is my fear of not having enough food to go around. Or perhaps I wish I was always feeding a long table of guests. Whatever it is, I love to batch-cook dishes or, more specifically, certain elements of them.

Having a loose plan for a mountain of cooked beans or grains (see pages 166–7) is helpful, to use them up in ingenious ways and with different toppings, as no one wants to feel they are eating the same thing night after night. I find joy in this reimagining of leftovers or certain ingredients, and fun in keeping things fresh and interesting.

Say you choose to batch-cook a ratatouille (see page 106). It can, of course, be served as is with a chunk of bread (and very nice it is, too). But add some cooked beans, chilli and cumin to take it on more of a bean chilli route, then serve it with rice, grated cheese and soured cream. Or use it as a pasta sauce. Or heat your ratatouille in a frying pan, maybe sprinkle in spices, then crack in a few eggs for a makeshift shakshuka. You see what I'm getting at. The only limit to leftovers or batch-cooks of food is, essentially, the imagination of the cook.

Batch-cooking is also amazingly economical with your time. It doesn't really take that much longer to make more of something; the ingredients still cook in stages, and you can still prep the vegetables as you go. It is an investment in your future meals. I love that feeling of getting home after a full-on day and remembering I have a hearty, healthy, nourishing bowl of food that needs only to be heated up in a pan.

It's important to make it enjoyable while you are batch-cooking, as well as merely happily anticipating the lessened stress and rushing around in the week that you'll have after you've got ahead. It's relaxing to set aside a couple of hours on a Sunday to cook food for the coming week, both in the process and in the contemplation of it. Or double-batch your Sunday dinner so that you can eat it again in a few days, giving you back some time later in the week. Put on your favourite podcast or some music or, to be honest, I just like the sound of the pans sizzling and bubbling away. It provides a bit of calm and quiet before the week begins.

Using the freezer in an organized way can be rewarding; squirrelling away a couple of containers of ready-cooked treasures for when you really need them is a kind gesture to your future self. I freeze cooked flatbreads or sliced muffins (see pages 45, 54, 65 and 46), then they only need to slot into the toaster at breakfast time. Equally, I will double-batch lentils or a stew, then seal half in a container and freeze it for when I need it most.

Equally, you can get ahead with bread dough. Make larger batches, chill it, then use it from the fridge over a few days. I tend to make dough in the evenings, then divide it into individual oiled sealable containers to prove. I leave it out overnight to prove if it is winter (it is very cold in our kitchen, but if the heating is on at your house, you may be best off refrigerating it), or in the fridge during the warmer months. It's a lovely feeling, knowing that you always have fresh dough on hand, slowly proving and developing flavour as it sits in the fridge.

Worthy? Perhaps. But batch-cooking will relieve the pressures of your working week and save time for your family. I'll take that.

INDEX

A
ajo blanco (sauce or soup) 58–9
asparagus & spinach with black olive breadcrumbs 192
aubergines 186, 188
  steamed aubergine with chilli-soy dressing 115

B
barley
  grain & veg traybake salad 134
  shortcut ratatouille sauce 106
basil pasta with peas & crunchy crumbs 199
batch cooking 204–5
beans
  baked rice with beans 139
  bean, tomato & red onion salad 18
  black bean & mushroom ma po 101
  black bean burgers 50
  brothy butter beans with steamed dumplings 38
  brothy shallots & butter beans with a herb crust 133
  butter beans with torn green olives, almonds & chilli 63
  cooking dried beans 166–7
  Hannah's rosemary pinto beans 82
  refried bean burritos 32
  sharp, speedy storecupboard bean salad 12
  stuffed yogurt flatbreads 65
bhel puri 24
broccoli 57
  broccoli & spelt hotcakes 98

C
cauliflower, baked buffalo 155
chard & Cheddar galettes 49
cheese
  baked Cheddar semolina with puttanesca sauce 143
  chard & Cheddar galettes 49
  Cheddar semolina, for summer 178
  cheesy French toast with sweetcorn salsa 89
  feta tart with tomato & olive salad 184–5
  filo baked feta with roast red pepper & cucumber salad 151
  goats' cheese polenta with spiced aubergines & dates 188
  onion cheese on toast 109
  oyster mushroom cheesesteaks with potato salad 174
  quesadillas 72
  rosemary & Cheddar soda bread scones 162
  squash & feta frittata 130
  sweet potato scarpaccia 191
chickpeas
  baked rice with chickpeas 138
  bhel puri 24
  buffalo chickpea crunch wrap 28
  chickpea curry with spinach theplas 177
  Georgian spiced spinach & chickpeas 112
  orecchiette with chickpeas 173
  polenta chips with saucy chickpeas 124
  speedy falafels 66
children 118–19
coconut & lime leaf broth with rice noodles 80
couscous
  crispy tofu, couscous, pickled onions & tzatziki 159
  jewelled couscous 10
curried tahini, lentil & crunchy veg salad 15

D
dumplings 16, 38, 91, 182, 196

E
eggs
  charred leeks, broken eggs, fried capers & dill 170
  crispy noodle omelette 69
  fried potato omelette with blue cheese 152
  squash & feta frittata 130
  'stir fry' fridge fritters 42
  sweet potato scarpaccia 191

F
falafels, speedy 66
fennel
  stuffed yogurt flatbreads 65
  tomato-fennel pasta with rocket 63
filo baked feta with roast red pepper & cucumber salad 151
flatbreads 72
  griddled olive, tomato & basil 45
  potato-stuffed flatbreads 54
  stuffed yogurt flatbreads 65
fussy eaters 118–19

G
garlic-chilli potato noodles 91
grain & veg traybake salad 134

H
hispi fatoush 23
hispi roasted with toasted seeds & crumbled chestnuts 126
hot sauce, canned fruit 75

K
kraut-loaded baked potatoes 137

L
leeks, broken eggs, fried capers, dill 170
lentils
  Austrian-style lentils with giant bread dumplings 182
  curried tahini, lentil & crunchy veg salad 15
  lentil cottage pie 156
  lentil, aubergine & potato bake 186

M
malthouse muffins 46
mushrooms
  baked mushroom parmigiana 129
  black bean & mushroom ma po 101
  creamy mushroom tofu broth with noodles 202

freeform mushroom lasagne 144
mushroom hotpot with herb
   dumplings 196
oyster mushroom cheesesteaks
   with potato salad 174
pickled shiitake sushi rice bowl 60
potted mushroom pâté 110

N

noodles
   coconut & lime leaf broth 80
   creamy mushroom tofu broth
      with noodles 202
   crispy noodle omelette 69
   silken tofu bun xa 27

O

olives 45, 63, 147, 192
   feta tart with tomato & olive
      salad 184–5
onions 18, 57
   brothy shallots & butter beans
      with a herb crust 133
   onion cheese on toast 109
   oven-baked onion bhajis 140
   roast onion soup with butter
      beans & olive-rosemary
      croutons 147
   speedy falafels 66

P

pasta
   asparagus & spinach with black
      olive breadcrumbs 192
   basil pasta with peas & crunchy
      crumbs 199
   freeform mushroom lasagne 144
   orecchiette with chickpeas 173
   squash minestrone 86
   squash pasta with toasted hazelnuts
      & crispy sage 181
   tomato-fennel pasta with
      rocket 53
peas
   monster pea & potato croquettes 70
   pea & potato pancakes with two
      chutneys 41
   peas-otto 97
   refried carlin peas 200

polenta
   baked polenta with creamed
      kale 161
   goats' cheese polenta with spiced
      aubergines & dates 188
   polenta chips with saucy
      chickpeas 124
potatoes
   fried potato omelette with blue
      cheese 152
   garlic-chilli potato noodles 91
   kraut-loaded baked potatoes 137
   lentil cottage pie 156
   lentil, aubergine & potato
      bake 186
   oyster mushroom cheesesteaks
      with potato salad 174
   pea & potato croquettes 70
   pea & potato pancakes 41
   potato-stuffed flatbreads 54
   tomato salad with smashed crispy
      potatoes & mojo verde 122

R

rice 60
   baked rice with beans 139
   baked rice with chickpeas 138
   squash & blue cheese risotto
      with toasted pecans & crispy
      sage 148
   sweetcorn fried rice 116
rocket salad 53
rosemary & Cheddar soda bread
   scones 162

S

seasoning 76–7
seed crackers 165
semolina
   baked Cheddar semolina with
      puttanesca sauce 143
   Cheddar semolina, for summer 178
sesame-crusted rice paper
   dumplings 16
spelt
   broccoli & spelt hotcakes 98
   spelt stew au pistou 85
   Tuscan spelt salad (autumn) 95
   Tuscan spelt salad (summer) 92

spinach 112, 192
   chickpea curry with spinach
      theplas 177
squash & blue cheese risotto
   with toasted pecans & crispy
   sage 148
squash & feta frittata 130
squash minestrone 86
squash pasta with toasted hazelnuts
   & crispy sage 181
squash saag 195
'stir fry' fridge fritters 42
storecupboard essentials 34–5
sweet potato & sweetcorn
   fritters 105
sweet potato scarpaccia 191
sweetcorn fried rice 116

T

tiger salad summer rolls with
   double-dunk sauce 20
tofu
   Chinese-style tomatoey tofu
      scramble 102
   creamy mushroom tofu broth
      with noodles 202
   crispy tofu, couscous, pickled
      onions & tzatziki 159
   silken tofu bun xa 27
   tofu with broken rice papers
      & spicy sauce 31
   whipped tofu with charred
      broccoli & red onion 57
tomatoes 18, 45, 102
   feta tart with tomato & olive
      salad 184–5
   stuffed yogurt flatbreads 65
   tomato salad with smashed crispy
      potatoes & mojo verde 122
   tomato-fennel pasta with
      rocket 53
tortillas, homemade 72

Y

yogurt
   stuffed yogurt flatbreads 65

ABOUT THE AUTHOR

Joe Woodhouse is author of the bestselling *Your Daily Veg* and *More Daily Veg*. He has been vegetarian since the age of 10, teaching himself how to cook, and later trained as a chef. He spent several years working in kitchens such as Vanilla Black and the Towpath Café, as well as contributing to events with restaurants such as The Quality Chop House in London. Alongside being a chef, he is also a photographer, shooting with clients such as Soho Farmhouse, Belazu, Marmite, Asda, Hakkasan and the Bold Bean Co. He is lauded among his colleagues – including Anna Jones and Nigella Lawson – for being one of the best vegetarian chefs in the business.

◉ joe_woodhouse

Recipe notes

- All the recipes mention 'sea salt'; a few mention 'sea salt flakes', when that is specifically what I mean. As a rule, though, I use fine sea salt for cooking and sea salt flakes for finishing dishes.
- When I use small amounts of flour – for binding a mixture, for instance, or in a bechamel – my default is plain white flour. But in these cases you could usually use whatever flour is in your cupboard, which is why in those cases I have just mentioned 'flour'.

UK/US TERMS

UK	US
Aubergines	Eggplants
Baking paper	Parchment paper
Barbecue	Grill
Bicarbonate of soda	Baking soda
Blanched nuts	Skinned nuts
Borlotti beans	Cranberry beans
Butter beans	Lima beans
Cannellini beans	White kidney beans
Cavolo nero	Tuscan kale
Cherry tomatoes	Grape tomatoes
Chestnut mushrooms	Cremini mushrooms
Chilli flakes	Red pepper flakes
Cider	Hard cider
Coriander (herb)	Cilantro
Cornflour	Cornstarch
Courgettes	Zucchini
Desiccated coconut	Unsweetened shredded coconut
Double cream	Heavy cream
Filo pastry	Phyllo dough
Fridge	Refrigerator
Frying pan	Skillet
Gherkins/cornichons	Pickles
Griddle pan	Grill pan
Grill	Broil/broiler
Groundnut oil	Peanut oil
Kitchen paper	Paper towels
Mature Cheddar cheese	Sharp cheddar cheese
Peppers	Bell peppers
Plain flour	All-purpose flour
Rocket	Arugula
Self-raising flour	Self-rising flour
Sieve	Strainer
Spring onions	Scallions
Stick blender	Immersion blender
Tomato purée	Tomato paste
Wholemeal	Wholewheat
Wild garlic	Ramps